MW00934524

WOMEN THRIVING FEARLESSLY!

Volume 1

Inspirational stories of women who

journeyed from fear to fearless

Other books available in the
Unstoppable Publishing's Library:

The Secrets to Being an Unstoppable Woman
Roll up your sleeves, make no excuses, and get what you want!

10 Ways to Prevent Failure (Audio Book)
A straightforward guide to help you stay focused on attaining your goals.

Starting Today
365 Quotations to stimulate, inspire, and enhance your personal growth.

The Unstoppable Woman's Guide to Emotional Well-Being
A book for women written by 23 female authors, coaches and professionals.

How to Write & Publish Your Book NOW!!
Step by step guide to put you on the fast track to becoming a published author.

Success Guide for the Unstoppable Entrepreneur
Straightforward guide to help new business owners and entrepreneurs excel in their business.

If You Leave, I Will Kill You! –
Getting Off the BEATEN Path of Domestic Violence

www.TheUnstoppableWoman.net

© **MMXV** All rights reserved. No part of this book may be reproduced or transmitted in any form or by any means, electronic or mechanical, including photocopying, recording, or by any information storage and retrieval system, without permission in writing from the author.

Illustrator: Arthur T. Pressley

TABLE OF CONTENTS

1

Too Prissy for That – My Double Life

Addie Ruth Wade - Taylor

 Ruth Wade-Taylor is a diligent, accomplished and talented individual who has worked in various organizations of the Federal Government for the past 20+ years. She is a native of Alabama. After graduating from high school, she relocated to Atlanta, Georgia. She has also served over 25 years in the Unites States Army Reserves, and has traveled extensively while serving in the military. Ruth's academic accomplishments include a Bachelor of Science Degree in Project Management from DeVry University, Decatur, Georgia. A Master of Business Administration in Human Resource Management from Keller Graduate School of Management, Decatur, Georgia, and Paralegal Specialist Course, Fort Jackson, South Carolina.

Ruth has held various leadership positions while serving in the United States Army Reserves: Senior Paralegal with the Staff Judge Advocate's Office, Personnel Services Specialist, Platoon Sergeant, Logistics, Food Service, and Administrative Non Commissioned Officer, (NCO). Ruth is an active member of the Society for Human Resource Management, (SHRM), and The National Society of Leadership and Success.

She resides in Georgia, with her husband Clifford. They are the proud parents of two beautiful adult daughters, Sherry Lynn and Zoie. Ruth and her husband are active in their church and community. They enjoy gardening, working in the yard, and participating in various activities such as the DAV 5K in honor of the veterans. For speaking engagements, Organizational Development training workshops, Veterans/Military seminars, SHRM conferences, she is available and will provide her services locally as well as nationally.

Post Office Box 82672
Conyers, Georgia 30013
Email: ruth.taylor987@gmail.com

Growing up in a small town of Seale, Alabama, I was a very quiet, and introverted child who stuttered a lot. However, that did not take away my dream of wanting to join the military and to follow in my father's footsteps of serving my country. Once I graduated from high school, I needed a job immediately, my oldest daughter was born on my high school graduation day, and I was not able to attend my high school graduation. My first job after high school was at a car wash in Columbus, Georgia, where my friend and I were both hired on the spot on the same day. After getting hired, we were excited at first. However, within a couple of hours, we looked at each other and we could clearly read each other's mind as we both knew that this was not the route we wanted to take in fulfilling our careers. It was then when I mentioned it to my friend and she was in agreement with me of joining the military on the buddy system. However, I had previously mentioned this to my family, and they had already ensured me that it would not work for me. As some of the responses to me were:

"Are you sure? You are too prissy for that."
"Now you know you are afraid of the dark."
"You know that you are afraid of spiders."

Actually, those reminders from friends and family were true, without a doubt. However, I was determined not to let it be a game changer for me, as joining the military was still on my list things that I wanted to fulfill.

That evening after work, I went home to discuss joining the military on the buddy system with my family, just to learn later, that one of my sisters had already joined the military. Again, I put my dreams on hold, as I did not want to leave our mother and smaller sisters home with both our kids to care for while me and my sister were away on military duty. My friend went along with our plans of discussion and enlisted in the military, and I was let go from the car wash.

What's the Point?

Several years passed, and I continued to have the heart to serve my country by enlisting in the United States Army Reserves. In August of 1980, this is when one of my dreams became a reality. I enlisted in the United States Army Reserves, and I had made up my mind did not discuss it with any of my family members or my friends because at that point my mind was made up and set on enlisting in the US Army. However, I did discuss my plans with my husband, although he did not take me too seriously. After all, I had taken the test at least twice and did not go thru with enlisting.

After enlisting in the Army Reserves, I actually had two lives; one as a soldier serving in the United States Army Reserves, and the other as a civilian Executive Administrative Assistant/Legal Instruments Examiner fulfilling my career with various jobs within the Federal Government.

I encountered various advantages and disadvantages while serving in the military. I also endured various challenges - namely being separated from family and friends during weekends and holidays. While serving in the military, I was also faced with various not so nice encounters in my civilian career with my supervisors. I'm not sure if it was because they were not abreast of the policy and procedures as a reservist being called to military duty, or if it was that they simply didn't care. I began my civilian career with the Federal Government in October of 1983. When I was offered to interview for the position, I was serving on a short tour of duty with my Army Reserves Unit, and

I interviewed for the position while in uniform. I informed the Agency that I was serving on active duty, and would not have time to go home and change for the interview, and was advised to come and interview in uniform. I interviewed and was offered the position and accepted. This was a high point in my life and my career, as I was doing what I enjoyed; starting my career with the Federal Government, working in the legal field, and serving in the United States Army Reserves. Both of my positions, my civilian job as well as my Army Reserve position, were equally fulfilling. Due to my position and unit's demands, I was called to duty both long tours as well as short tours quite often from my civilian job. Shortly after being hired at the Agency, I was called up for a six month tour of duty with my Unit, 3rd Medical Command. My Supervisor informed me that if I left my civilian job for a six month military tour of duty, after its completion I would not have the privileges that I have now, and I would be treated as if I was a new employee all over again. I had no choice but to accept his demands, rules and regulations when I returned.

The policies were requiring the last employee hired would carry out the duties such as Mail Clerk, Receptionist and others duties and responsibilities that were not in the scope of the Legal Instruments Examiner's job description, while at the same time, maintain the caseload of your assigned attorney.

While serving on this tour of duty with my Reserve Unit, my civilian supervisor, the Agency attorney, sent a letter to my Unit Commander asking that I be relieved of my military duties because I was needed at the office. A copy of this letter was given to me by another soldier who worked in the administrative section. However, I did not follow up with questions, and it was never addressed to me. After my tour of duty, I returned to work at my civilian job, and performed the duties as a newly hired employee, as were outlined by the policies of the Agency.

While being employed at the Agency, due to mistreatment, poor career advancement and promotion opportunities, a class action suit was filed. Even though I was a part of the class action suit, I was not afforded the settlement that was granted to the other employees.

I relocated to Texas due to my husband's military assignment. Usually, when my husband got relocation military assignments, I would not relocate with him. Instead, I remained at our home base, in Atlanta, Georgia, and continued my double life as a Federal Government Employee, and an Army Reservist. However, when the assignment orders came for him to relocate to Abilene, Texas, we both realized that this was not a weekend trip for traveling back and forth. We prayed on this situation for clarity and direction, then we discussed the situation and prayed some more. This was a very difficult decision for us to make because we had a very young child at that time. I did not want to deprive my husband of the growing years of our daughter even though we were married for fifteen years before having a child. However, after praying, fasting, discussing the situation among ourselves, and listening to friends giving their advice, one day in a quiet voice, I heard these words, "The same God that took care of you here in Atlanta, will take care of you in Texas." I immediately discussed it with my husband and informed him that we (me and our 2 ½ year old daughter) will be relocating to Texas as a family.

In October of 1999, I began furthering my career with the Federal Government back to Atlanta. This is when I began to work with another Federal Agency. Again, I was very excited about my double life and careers with my civilian job as well as with serving in the Army Reserves. At one point, I had to file an Equal Employee Opportunity (EEO) complaint when I returned to my civilian job from a military assignment. One thing that I learned from this endeavor is that you have to be mentally, physically, and emotionally fit to take on a task like this because you will have to convince them that the issues that you are alleging did in fact happen. It was also a big challenge asking for co-workers to give a statement on my behalf, indicating that the issues that I was alleging did in fact happen because they were afraid that they would be harassed or even lose their jobs as well. My closest friend and coworker at the time, simply said to me, "Ruth, I do not want to get involved, because I need my job, and my husband has advised me not to." I accepted her honesty. However, that just convinced me to continue to fight for what was right, and it made me even stronger.

There were some days when I left work in tears after being verbally beat down by my peers. I'd go home and cry and pray all night long, and the next day, return to work looking fresh and prissy. At that point, the only thing that I could do was to trust and believe, read, meditate, and quote scriptures. One scripture in particular that got me thru this ordeal was and still is Deuteronomy 31:6-7, New King James Version, (NKJV), "Be strong and of good courage, do not fear nor be afraid of them; for the Lord your God, he is the One who goes with you. He will not leave you nor forsake you." This scripture really encouraged me to continue on with both of my careers. However, during this season of my life, it was not an easy one for me; I faced depression, had to seek counseling, and seek assistance from a psychiatrist as well. On my civilian job, I was so depressed from the treatment that I received from my supervisors while away on military duty, as well as when I returned to my civilian job. On one occasion, when I was called to military duty, I remember I had an appointment with my psychiatrist. I called him to inform him that I would not be able to attend my appointment but I wanted to reschedule for when I returned. He said to me, "Well you better be ready to put on your boxing gloves when you return to work then." I was not really sure of what he meant by that comment. I do know that it was confirmation to me that this person did not have my interest at heart. When I returned, I sought the assistance from another doctor instead of the employee recommended doctor.

During my military career as a reservist and active duty, I missed some of the holidays with friends and family. However, I was and am truly blessed with a wonderful husband who carried on the daily household chores while I was away on duty. One time in particular, I remember going on our Annual Training (AT) and at this particular time our youngest daughter, Zoie, was only three months old. Although it was hard to leave my three month old baby girl for a military duty assignment, I knew that she would be cared for with love and care from her dad.

Though there were many advantages and disadvantages during my tour of duty in the military, I can truly say that for me, staying the course really outweighed the disadvantages of being female in the military in several ways, namely:

- The majority of my college tuition was paid for with my military benefits such as Post 9/11
- I earned my Bachelors of Arts Degree in Project Management
- In 2014, I earned my Masters of Business Administration, (MBA) in Human Resources

- I was afforded the opportunity to travel and see the world by joining the military
- Met friends from all walks of life
- Medical benefits

One challenge that I faced while in the military was on one of my military tours of duty. My supervisor sent me on the advance party to the Middle East with all male soldiers. I felt that it was not completely the right thing to do because I was always taught accountability, travel in pairs, etc., and this was not the case. However, we completed our mission, and this was a learning experience for me. In some instances, sometimes you have to do what you have to do in order to save your career. Once we arrived, and was issued the vehicles to drive back and forth to our work site and pick up daily mail, we discovered that none of the male soldiers on this tour of duty knew how to drive a manual transmission vehicle. However, I knew how to operate one because at the time, this was all I could afford to drive in the civilian world. Therefore, it was my duty to give a lesson to the male soldiers on this task so that our daily tasks could be evenly distributed. As I stated earlier, I was the only female soldier sent on the Advance Party (a group that is sent ahead of the main body to set up and perform reconnaissance before the main body arrives) on this tour of duty, and when we were all retiring for the night, I went to my building for the night. I looked up on the roof and I saw foreign soldiers peeping down into my building. Whatever the reason, I was not planning to stay the night in my building until the main body of soldiers arrived. Therefore, I went to my Sergeant Major to advise him of the situation. He listened, understood, and he allowed me to place my cart up front in their building with my Advance Party male soldiers. For every problem that arises in your life, there is a solution for it, and this was the solution to this issue.

In 2004, I was on a military duty assignment to Fort Jackson, SC, for a reclassification class of 27D (Delta), due to a new position that I was in, which at the time was identified as the hardest and intense class that was being taught at the school. I graduated from the class. While there, I was continually harassed by my civilian supervisor, calling and asking me when my return date to work was even though I had turned in my orders to the appropriate staff before departing for duty. Trying to study for the class, and dealing with trying to hold down my civilian job was beginning to be very stressful for me. However, at the time, I was not abreast of the policy and procedures of who to contact for assistance; I just knew that I wanted to do the correct thing.

After returning from one of my military tours of duty in 2004, I was continually harassed by my supervisor and upper management on my civilian job. It was after the return of a military tour of duty is when the problems and issues really began. It was never mentioned by my supervisors that this was the main reason. Being in the military as well as my career on my civilian job was very difficult at times. However, I had no choice but to stay the course, pray, and keep the faith that things would eventually get better.

During my last tour of duty in 2004, (which was approximately four months) in Fort Jackson, South Carolina, one morning while performing Physical Training (PT), I fell and hurt both my knees approximately a week before my tour ended. I was treated at the facility, and was advised to follow up with my unit when I returned to my home station reserve unit because I needed follow up care and treatment. However, when I returned to my home unit and provided the papers for the follow up medical treatment, nobody seemed to have known the proper procedures to follow. Thus, this caused me to be denied medical treatment as well as being put on proper extended orders due to the lack of knowledge or proper procedures that was to be followed by my superiors. Therefore, because of the lack of knowledge and no one took on the task of accelerating my needs, I had no choice but to return to work on my civilian job while I was in pain with my knees. After returning to work to my civilian employer, and not being fully recovered from the knee injuries I suffered while on active duty, I made an appointment with my primary physician to seek medical assistant for my knees. My primary physician advised follow-up appointments and physical therapy, which caused me to take a vast amount of time off from my civilian job. While doing this, it caused issues with my civilian employer, which involved being denied leave, denied promotions, low performance appraisals, blame games, and being harassed by supervisor. At one point, it got so severe until I had to seek employee counseling. However, this did not suffice, and my next step was arbitration, which did not suffice, and my last resort was to file an EEO Complaint. When initiating an EEO Complaint, you (the complainant) have to be both physically and mentally ready for this journey because in most cases, as was in mine, I lost friends as well as being treated differently by co-workers and supervisors.

At one point during this process, the stress was so intense until it caused me to go into deep depression and having anxiety attacks. While being treated by my primary physician, he advised and referred me to seek assistant from a doctor of psychiatry and a counselor, which I sought. Bear in mind that during this time while seeking medical assistance, I am still in physical therapy and going to medical appointments for my knees. But I did not get the medical treatment for an injury that was incurred while on active duty until years later. After going thru these obstacles with both my civilian and military career, I was advised by my civilian doctor that the remedy for my healing was to let all of these issues go; do not check my emails, and was ordered to take six weeks leave of absence from my civilian job. After that, I was not getting any better and was advised to continue the leave until I had gotten better. At this point, I was beginning to think that things could not get any worse for me, and if so, how was I going to sustain it. However, at this point, things did turn for the worse for me, I was no longer able to perform my military duties because of my knee injury. It was difficult for me to sit for long periods of time, stand for long periods of time, and I could not jump into the foxholes as it was required for my duty position. In essence, I was physically incapable of reasonably performing my duties as a 27D Legal Specialist. Again, this was in line with no one being knowledgeable of the proper procedures and policies of taking care of an injured soldier while on active duty. Because of this, I was medically discharged from the military, because of an injury that I sustained from the military, and proper procedures not be followed. Parallel with this, I had no choice but to retire from my civilian job.

However, in the midst of all of what I was going through, there was an angel in the mist of my storm no matter what the circumstance. When you think there is no right answer, or assistance, I can truly say that I overcame the obstacles that I was facing, as I never gave up.

After crying, praying, and searching or looking for pity, I began to get up and do something for myself. I enrolled in college, and earned my MBA, Masters of Business Administration, in Human Resources. In summary, I encourage you to never give up, always keep a "can-do" attitude, follow your dreams, and the rest will fall in place.

2

Single Mom, Reinvented

Adrienne Stevens

 Adrienne found her niche in individual tax preparation as an undergraduate at Robert Morris College now known as Robert Morris University. She began working at H&R Block in 1997 and discovered the flexibility of the company fit well with the demands of her accelerated academic career and in the future, raising a son. While caring for a toddler, she managed to begin the Master of Accountancy program at DePaul University which she completed in 2008. As a working single mother, Adrienne understands the value of prioritizing tasks, being disciplined, and relying on God in order to thrive fearlessly.

Contact info: astevenspro@gmail.com
Please include *Women Thriving Fearlessly* as the subject

Hot tears run down my cheeks only to evaporate quickly in the chilly Chicago autumn night wind. Why am I walking the streets of Rogers Park alone in the middle of night sobbing, gasping for air as my mind races on how I can escape this trap that I deliberately created for myself?

I have to get away, but I'm so tired. I don't have a job. I have very little money. My breasts begin to ache...oh, I also have a newborn son. He's probably getting hungry. My husband is on house arrest and I'm positive that is the only reason he is still at home. Who will take care of that beautiful little baby if I run away? Would he raise him? Could he raise him? That was always the plan. My good friend and I wanted boys so if our husbands acted up, they could raise the child and we could continue our careers. There's only one problem with that theory: I am the mommy. "I'm the mommy. I'm the Mommy! I'M THE MOMMY!!!!?" What was I thinking? I must get home and feed my son.

I wanted him. I *asked* for him. Ever since our first planned pregnancy three years ago, I've been dreaming of a boy named Jacob and I got exactly what I wanted: a beautiful, healthy, baby boy. I read to him in the womb, and I rubbed the bottoms of his feet often, so I was sure he was going to be smart. My other request during my daily prayers was that this child make it to the end of the term. Not only to avoid the devastation of a miscarriage, but for the joy of holding a cute little baby who will stop crying immediately when picked up by his mommy.

Now worrying about the outcome of my marriage, how I will support this child, and my obvious lack of emotional well-being, has me looking for the door. It hasn't even been a week since he was born. I took some deep breaths. I told myself that I'll figure it out somehow. I'll pray and I'll talk to my family. I'll give him extra hugs and kisses, so he'll never get the inclination that I was ready to leave him. After all, he is *my* son. He is *my* responsibility. He is my *heart*. I put my key in the door and unlocked my future.

Two days later, I'm officially alone with my five-day old son. My husband has decided jail would be better than living with the crazy person I'd become. I have to focus on caring for my child. I discover the miracle of a swing and am able to nap. One of the first times I woke up from a nap, I panicked because he was not in my bed. Surely, someone stole him! It was probably that cartoon character that stalked around on his tippy-toes! No, he was in the swing. But where was my mind? Do other people go through this? I always wanted to be married before I had a baby and now I still find myself all alone I saw something that looked like a rat the other day. I need help. I need to make sure my baby will be safe. What can I do? I have to find a better living situation. I have to find a way to support us. I have to maintain my joy. And I have to do it all *NOW*.

I'm not proud of that night of desperation. I cringe at even considering abandoning my son. However, that was ten minutes of my life and I'm proud I came back, proud that I breastfed, that I moved to the suburbs with my grandmother and surrounded my child with love and positive people. I made a choice to marry the man I married and to have a baby. I couldn't force him to be responsible no matter how convinced I was of his love. I accepted my role with a polar mix of apprehension and determination, stumbled upon the courage I needed to make the necessary changes in my life, and discovered the ecstasy that can exist in motherhood.

It wasn't always rainbows and three years later, I found myself back in the city with the beautiful creature you see here. Isn't he precious? Do you feel like you know him? Maybe even love him a little? There were times when I did not. In my selfishness and immaturity, I would allow myself to be overwhelmed by the burden of the cooking, cleaning the house, cleaning "the kid", protecting "the kid", teaching "the kid", entertaining "the kid" and everything else that came with this *job.* One day when he was being less than cooperative I shouted "I hate you!" Let me take a moment to say that it is not automatically in a child's job description to be cooperative.

In order to be a good parent, you must learn about the stages of development during childhood. Although ashamed of my outburst, I thought he was young enough where it would not do any permanent damage. To compensate for my immediate guilt, I patiently completed whatever task had frustrated me to the point of that insanity and continued on with our day. Less than a week a later, we were out with a friend and apparently it was I who was not cooperating this time and my son shouted "I hate you!" to me!

My friend was appalled! She let out a gasp and told him to never say that again. I was embarrassed, not because of what he said, but because of the source from where he learned the phrase. I was glad that she did not have children and seemed unaware that I had anything to do with his new vocabulary, but I knew.

There was nothing for me to do, but learn the lesson and move on with life. I am proud to say I never used the phrase again.

Why had it come to this? I had just come off of working 35 hours a week, plus attending night school to earn a master's degree and all I saw was the work I was putting in to support my little family. The time spent after work was not quality time admiring the new discoveries and achievements my young one was making. I didn't even realize how quickly a three-year old could pick up on phrases and use them in the correct situation. I realized that I needed to really spend time with my son if I was going to appreciate him. I had already begun my hustle of even higher education just to support us. I sometimes felt like I was part of a covert operation when I was sneaking him into the university's computer lab to complete assignments. Thank goodness for pbskids.org!

My husband had been in and out of our lives. In a 2012 Pew Research survey, 65% of the respondents felt that children are better off when a parent stays home. This was definitely true in my case. I decided that spending as much time as possible with my son was what *I* needed in order to value him as a person and my role as a mother, so from May-December, that is what I did. It was an enlightening, mostly relaxed, and pleasant time and I wouldn't change that experience for the world.

School was nearing its end and so was my lease that was not going to be renewed. Once again, I needed a way to support us and a place to live. I went in for an interview for a job in the western suburbs. It was the only offer and it was for a temporary position. I was currently living in Rogers Park, my son still attended preschool at a magnet school on the south side of Chicago, and I didn't have a car.

The company decided that my offer should be for a permanent position and I accepted. We got up at 4 in the morning, sleeping on the two buses and the train to the southside to get him to the daycare. Then I would take another two trains to get to my job by 8:45a.m., fifteen minutes late, every day, but it could not be avoided. Then I would leave at 4:45 to repeat the reverse process, somehow feed and wash us both, and be in bed by 8:30 cursing anyone who disturbed my much-needed sleep. How was this going to work? Fortunately, there was lots of cuddling on the cold public transportation and I would use the evenings to read to him and have him tell me about his day. How I appreciated my decision not to work the prior summer to build a better foundation with my son! Still, within two weeks, with a lot of help, I found an apartment a block away from work, a nice daycare provider, and a car. We would walk around our quiet suburb admiring the beautiful lights of the winter season, play board games, and watch movies. It was better than I could have foreseen. It may have seemed rash to take that job offer, but I still live in that quaint part of town where the neighbors say "hi" on the prairie path and teachers greet you at the deli. I am proud I had the courage to take a chance when I didn't have all the answers and it has inspired me time and time again to do it again.

The next decision was not so impulsive, but was equally exhausting from an emotional standpoint. Should I divorce? It was my husband's second term in prison since we'd gotten married. Was I a failure? Did I not have enough faith? Enough love? Was I only focusing on the bad? Surely, the list was long enough. Finally, it was the realization that I could not make him be responsible. I could not make him be a stable and positive influence in my son's life. That was something he'd have to do on his own and if he really wanted to, it would be his own love and not my constant direction that would enable him to do so. He was not currently in a situation to be that person and it was painfully obvious that the past couple of years were just a provision of mounting evidence I could not change him. I filed the paperwork in my county and less than six years after our vow til death, we were both very much alive and divorced. I was not going to waste more good years. To my surprise, shortly after his release I received an e-mail stating that he had divorced me in the county which he lived. Due to the volatile nature of our relationship, I feared telling him of my filing so he had no clue that we were already divorced. I left it that way.

I began dating a couple of years earlier. Mostly it was taking my son to various places of amusement I could not afford and then having dinner. A great source of companionship was someone from my past. It was good to have someone I loved and trusted dolt on my son and take us places. One night, he stayed over and we fell asleep. It was the middle of winter and he lived a few hours away. He went to warm his car up and prepared to leave while it was still dark in order to arrive to work on time. I went back to sleep. Suddenly, he was in my room carrying my son. He put him in the bed with me. My son was cold. He said he found him walking around my building, but at first I couldn't understand the words coming out of his mouth. I couldn't breathe. My son was cold. He was outside? In the wee hours of the morning? For how long? I held him close and asked him why he left the house. He said he had a bad dream and when he woke up he heard the front door close, so he got up to follow me and find me... in the middle of the night, in his underwear! See, my son did not expect someone else to be here in the night. When he heard the door, he had no precedent to consider the possibility that it could be someone else leaving. He could have gotten kidnapped, sick, hit by a car...the what ifs still haunt me. I cried and cried and cried. This was not how I wanted to live my life.

For a time, I could only think about all that I'd be giving up if I stopped dating. Life outside of work had become almost constant entertainment, shopping, and dining out. We are both still recovering from the effects of my hedonistic lifestyle. This way of living did not reflect my true values. I kept telling myself it was temporary. I told myself that for years. My son was getting older and I didn't want him to see me going out with different men. I wanted him to have a relationship with God and I wanted to lead by example. For my future and my son's future, I changed my number. That was the easy part. Drawing closer to God and learning to rely on Him, that takes time and effort, but it is so worth it! We have a solid foundation to guide us and help us resolve whatever problems come our way. My son reads the Bible every day, he volunteers weekly to bring its message to others, and he made a personal decision at 12 years old to be baptized. I am so proud of him.

Over the years we have received a lot of help and I have tried to be there for my family and help them as well. Sometimes this involved letting a relative stay with us. One thing I've learned is not to let other people have the final decision on how I parent. I've struggled with trying to prove how tough I could be on occasion, but what a child needs most is attention, clear and consistent direction, and to feel loved and understood. At times I am still surprised at how important I am to my son. I'll never forget what it took for him to realize he was important to me.

A trusted relative was staying with us and we decided to go to the park district and play basketball to relieve some stress. I went down to the car, leaving my son upstairs. When they both got in the car, I could immediately feel that something was wrong. They were both quiet and I figured there must have been some sort of argument.

Something catches my attention as I walk in the gym with my son. I stop him. I look at his face. Is there just a hint of red around his eye? I ask him what is wrong with his face and his words hit me like a gunshot. He had been punched in the face! I gasped, then I spun around, "you hit him?!" I screamed. "No, I didn't!" was the reply. I pictured myself raining down blows myself, but was blinded by the tears as I grabbed my son's hand and said we had to go. I was almost hysterical in the car. My son's face is turning colors and this person had the audacity to lie and say they didn't do it?! Flashbacks of my marriage did not help the situation. I wanted to fight or at least call the police, but I imagined them asking why a two-time felon convicted of violent crimes was alone with my son in the first place? I felt nauseous. I let them get out of the car and quickly got in the driver's seat and sped off. First, I needed to get my son an ice pack. Then we needed a plan. I felt so betrayed and confused. I never imagined this would happen. Was this the first time? Why hadn't my son told me right away?

I decided to make some phone calls. I called three people who cared about us and could be objective. Then I called a locksmith. I sat in the car and waited. I told my son this was not his fault and never be afraid to say someone hurt him. There's a difference between getting help and being a snitch. I had him stay in the car as I went up with the locksmith. They were still packing and shocked to see what I was doing. They were crying and apologizing and saying it wasn't necessary to change the locks, but I hadn't lived my life on paper until then. Living life on paper means making decisions solely based on facts and not emotion.

On paper, this person should not have lived with us. On paper, this person should not have been alone with my son. On paper, this would never have happened. I was going to live on paper now. On paper, they had to go. The next evening, my son and I were having dinner and he said "now I know I am more important to you" and for the second time in twenty-four hours, my heart broke.

A few years passed and the environment at my job was becoming increasingly toxic. I noticed a decline in my and my coworker's personality. I found myself imitating the very traits I had come to detest and again it was my child who was suffering. Each summer I attend a three day religious convention and for many years I would return to work convinced that I had to find another job. Yet, there were many conveniences of where I worked. After one convention, I called my mom to discuss my concerns. The depravity of the people in charge had affected my spirituality and I no longer wanted my son to be with me at work. She said to try to have another job lined up before I quit and gave me some websites to use in my job search. It is difficult to search for a job while working full-time, but I did find a couple of leads.

One was in my current profession and one was not. Both were temporary. I prayed and gave myself a deadline. As the date approached, I had not solidified either position and could only find the time to do so after the deadline. Undeterred and with faith that I was making the right decision for the right reasons, I quit my job. The next day, I interviewed for a position in my current profession and I got the job! It would start in three months and it was still temporary, scheduled to last only 4 months. The next day I interviewed with a catalog company.

I had learned a little more about the available positions the week before and knew it paid substantially less than what I was accustomed to earning, but during the interview I realized that in my eagerness I had not paid attention to one small detail...the required hours. I had been so proud of myself, when the interviewer said she would get back to me I was assertive and told her I was told I would have an answer that day so that I could take the drug test and start on Monday. She went and discussed it with her supervisor and came back and offered me the job, from 7am to 7pm, Monday-Friday. My mind began to race. Somehow I had formed the idea that I could choose an eight-hour period within that time frame! "I'm about to cry", I said. She excused herself suggesting maybe I call my husband, but there wasn't one. This job was an hour away from my home. It was only temporary. Maybe I could spend a quality hour with Jacob before he went to bed. Then I remembered the religious meetings I take him to on Thursday nights. Nothing should interfere with that. The decision was made. I had to decline. The tears dried up and a calm came upon me. Someone in the elevator commented that things must have went well. I replied that they hadn't, but I knew I had made the right choice. While driving home, I got a call offering me another position with the company with more reasonable hours. My faith has resulted in many blessings. My temporary job became a permanent, salaried position that allows me to homeschool my son. We are closer and happier and more fulfilled.

Wherever you are on life's journey, it is not too late to change your course. Rely on God, and He will make your path straight.

3

From the Bitter Ashes, SHE STEPPED!

Annette Whittington

Physically, mentally and sexually abused as a young child by the people who were entrusted to care for her, Annette Whittington has become an advocate for children. She is passionate about bringing her personal message of survival and healing from childhood abuse to now being an Intentional Parenting Coach and Youth Coach. Abandoned by her mother as an infant, Annette was raised by her grandmother, who had no clue that she had evil living in her house. And it was in her Grandmother's home that Annette kept a secret that almost destroyed her life.

Annette is an elected School Board Member of District 205, Thornton Township High School. She is a Certified John Maxwell Speaker, Teacher and Coach. She is a Certified Vision board Facilitator, and a Mental Health Advocate. She is a wife, mother, grandmother, and sister who is passionate about life. She resides in the south suburbs of Illinois and is happily married to her husband who is Alderman of their town. She works to share techniques with parents that empower them to sow seed of greatness into the lives of their children so that they can become great. Annette has travel worldwide as far as Ghana West Africa to bring her message.

Annette Whittington
Website: www.Be-An-Intentional-Parent.com
Facebook: www.facebook.com/beanintentionalparent
Twitter: @ann_whittington

I felt as if I had reached my breaking point...the tears would not stop flowing...the pain was excruciating...my body was numb all over...I felt like my heart and mind were going to explode and I couldn't shake the feeling of misery and hopelessness. I screamed, I cried. "I'm going to hell, I'm going to die, God, please help me!!!" I dropped into a heap of despair on the floor curling into a fetal position.

Have you ever experienced a sense of helplessness; a sense of being trapped.... Remember YOU are the master of your destiny. At age 42, with a devoted husband, an awesome daughter, and wonderful twin boys, I was blessed. It seems that I had everything to live for, but my mind was consumed with negative thoughts. They adored me; I was a good mother and wife, always putting my family first. But yet on most days I felt as if I had reached the end of my rope. On a normal day you couldn't look at me and tell that my mind was in pain. I had literally lost a desire to live (I could wear my mask well). But inside I was dying a slow death, falling deeper and deeper into a dark black hole of depression.

I did genuinely love my family, and I had so much to be thankful for. After all, my husband did marry me after a courtship of only three weeks and I'm now proud to say this is my 25th year of marital bliss. (Only God knew my Joseph Whittington would be able to tolerate a broken woman like me). My 36-year old daughter cherished me in spite of my wild single life, when I had no idea what parenting was. My 23-year old twin boys, Jeremiah and Nathaniel were born a miracle. The doctors told us to expect the worst as they wouldn't survive and even suggested selective abortion; they wanted to take one so the other could survive. But... every day my low self-esteem haunted me day and night with words I took to be true:

"Look, at you Annette, you're ugly, and you are stupid"
"You are a loser and you never do anything right"
"You are always losing stuff and you are always running late"
"You'll never amount to anything; you're worthless"
"Why do you even try?
"Don't you know your family would be better without you?"

I loved my family but the hurt felt like a dagger going through my heart. I'd ask myself constantly, "What is wrong with me?" What did I do to deserve this?"

My sub-conscious thoughts thrived on my volatile beginning. I was born out of wedlock on March 22, 1959 in Minneapolis, Minnesota to Ruth Huff and Andrew Jarrett. I was the fourth of five children birthed by a mother who could not parent because of her low self-esteem and she gave her five babies away to be cared by different friends and relatives. I remember faint images of my mother, but my strongest feelings said to me that I was not good enough for her love. I remember crying myself to sleep at night saying, "If she loved me, she never would have left me and if my mother can't love me, no one else will." My life began not having the love and warmth of my mommy.

Being unloved and unwanted was further confirmed in my spirit by my father who was a very mean-spirited man who would relentlessly tell me that "I was just like my no good mother" and I would "never amount to anything in life." His definition of love was dependent on "good behavior" and conditional love. I grew up feeling like I never quite reached his standards. I felt rejected by my father who I loved. If I could do things exactly the way he wanted it, then I would have his love. If I didn't, then I was called stupid and dumb and ignorant. My prayer was that he would love me and be proud of me, but I don't think he ever knew how to. But my spirit blamed me. And I was destined for destruction even before I was even conceived.

I will never forget that on January 15, 2002, I woke up late again and with only 30 minutes to get out of the house. I quickly put on jeans, splashed water on my face, brushed my teeth, threw on a scarf, rambled for my keys and ran out the house. Running late AGAIN to work, (that was my norm) and with no time to waste. It was always a race with the clock and I was always the one to lose.

"Get up Annette, you've got to put on your 'fake happy face.'" You have two beautiful babies depending on you. You have a beautiful teenage daughter and a loving husband. What would they say if you just lay in bed all day? "Time to get up, Annette." My fear was that I would let my family down if they knew that I usually cried myself to sleep praying that tomorrow would never come, wishing away the sunshine. If my family knew I really didn't want to live anymore, if my friends really knew that I didn't have it together what would they say?

Finally, after a long day at work as a customer service rep listening to customers one after another complain about their bill and trying to resolve their issue in my little sweet voice, the clock finally struck 5pm and it was time to leave this rat race of a job. Working in a call center behind headsets, I had gotten good at wearing a mask so no one would know my internal pain. I quickly got to my car anxiously thinking about the cigarettes and joint that would help me relax on that long drive home. I hated going home. My husband and I didn't get along and we never spoke to each other without a hostile tone of voice and my kids were always so needy. So usually after dinner I left the house to sneak a cigarette and joint in the comfort of my car. My husband would always love me unconditionally, but I had no idea what REAL LOVE was about and the more he tried to love me, the harder I pushed him away.

As I warmed up my car to leave the parking lot of my job, my cell phone rang. From the caller ID I could see that it was my step-mom, who I claim as my "Angel." Suddenly I had a flashback of the day my dad pulled a gun out on us and accused us of stealing his money. I was 13 at the time, and if it had not been for my grandmother ringing the doorbell at that very second, I am sure we would have been shot. Whenever my step-mom called, I was quick to answer because I never knew her current situation. "Hey Ma-Dear," which is what I called her, "How you doing?" "I'm good, Honey," she replied. "Did you pay that car note last month? Because I got a notice in the mail that it was late. Well actually your Dad saw the notice and I want to let you know he is on the warpath. He wants you to stop by here on your way home." I told her I really did not want to talk to him and that as soon as I got my paycheck on Friday, I would pay it. She said, "I know honey, but you know how your Dad is; he will find anything to start arguing about. Just call him and tell him that you are going to pay it on Friday, so I don't have to hear his fussing." I told her "Ok," but I knew in my heart that it was something that I could not do. Suddenly, I felt as if I was about to have a heart-attack. My heart began to pound, but I kept my voice calm and reassured her I would call him when I got home, but I just couldn't come by and face him.

As the story goes, my step-mom had co-signed for a car for my daughter who was in college. However, my daughter had recently lost her job and was unable to make the scheduled payment. I had promised my step-mom when the car was purchased that if my daughter ever got in a jam that I would make sure the car note was paid on time. But times had been rough for us financially and I had fallen behind on the payments. Again, I thought I was being misunderstood and judged as dumb and ignorant.

As I drove along the freeway toward home, the negative flashbacks started, and a flurry of mixed emotions gripped me. I instantly saw myself as the little 4 years old girl who always made the wrong decisions. I saw myself as the mischievous child at 5 who cut her hair for attention but was misunderstood and ran away from home for fear of being beaten. I saw myself as that little girl who was found swinging in the park then dragged home and beaten even harder because I had run away for fear of harsh punishment. I remember no one ever asked why I ran away or even cared. They just assumed that I was being bad. I sadly remembered the girl who used to lose her gloves on the way to school and as a punishment, was put in the closet with no food. I suddenly felt like I was that 4 year girl old again, who was being molested but told it was all my fault. I felt like the little girl who grew up thinking that my mommy left because she did not love me and because I was ugly and had nappy hair. I felt like that normal 16 year old who wanted to have a date for the dance at school and when I was told no, I sneaked out anyway. When my daddy found out, I got a black eye and was put out of the house at 2am wandering the streets hiding in bushes because I was afraid and misunderstood. I felt like the 21 year old who got pregnant because I wanted someone to love me, but when I had the baby I dumped her for a man who said he loved me but all he wanted was to turn me into a prostitute because I was easy and would do anything just for love. I was tired of being misunderstood and at that point I just wanted out of life.

The tears came so fast that I barely could see the road. I finally made my way off of the interstate and pulled over to the street next on top of the overpass. I sat there for a moment wishing that God would help me out of this situation, as I had no idea what I was going to tell my dad. I just knew I did not have the money, and I just could not confront him because I would be misunderstood, AGAIN. I could not take him cussing me out AGAIN. So I just sat there crying, praying, and contemplating what to do. I knew I had to face him sooner or later, but for now I felt like a small scared child. I knew I had to call because if I didn't he would take it out on my step mom. I asked myself, "Why should I keep going on with life and living a lie? It is only going to get worse. Nobody loves me and they won't miss me. Why? Because I am no good to or for my family. I'll never be good enough because I can never do anything right." Those were the negative words that played over and over in my mind as I sat in my car, shaking and crying. At that moment, at the age of 42, the thought of suicide took over my mind and the negative voices grew so loudly that any voice of hope was drowned out. So many times prior, I had pleaded with my husband to have me committed to a mental institution. "I'm not good for you, and the kids will be better off without me." So many times I remember him coaxing me out of a fetal position in the corner where I went to feel safe, away from the touch of human love. And here I was again contemplating suicide.

I remember getting out of my car and walking to bridge over the interstate and looking down at the cars whizzing by below. All it would take would be a quick jump and it would be all over with. Quick, fast, and in a hurry. I could feel my heart beating fast like

I was in a race against time. There was a lump in my throat making it almost impossible to shallow. My eyes were in a trance and all I could think about was, "I can't take it anymore, I am so tired. I want it over now. My heart was hurting so bad....and for a moment my only thought was death by suicide."

Then I heard God's voice say, "Surrender and Trust. You shall live and not die." I remember at that point falling to my knees right there on the concrete and crying out and asking God to help me. I had lived 42 years battling low self-esteem and a sense of personal failure and I was tired. I was bullied and beat up during my elementary school days, but I had endured it. I had been teased during my middle school years, but I endured it. I was an outcast during my high school years, but I had endured it. I had been rejected during college and ended up dropping out because I was misunderstood. My own father had kicked me out of the house when my baby was just first born.

I remember believing these lies about myself my whole 42 years, but now here was God whispering to me that, "His plans for my life were greater than my plans." But the pain was so unbearable for me that I just wanted to give up. But I heard God's voice again say, "I am here with you, do not be afraid, for I love you unconditionally and there is greatness within you. You shall live and not die."

I will forever be grateful for that moment of self-destruction  because it actually was a moment of self-awareness. My depression was the beginning of a new life of self-awareness. My pain that night served a purpose. It showed me that there is nothing [no thing] that God will not do if we will only trust Him. God closed my mind for that moment to the lies that were buried in my subconscious, and I became aware of the enemy that was trying to destroy me. At that moment I took action to live and not die.

That night with my best girlfriend and my husband by my side, we went to the hospital where I admitted that I needed help because I tried to kill myself. The first step in healing is to love yourself enough to admit that you are powerless and at that moment you surrender to a higher power. My loved ones confirmed that I had been hurting for many years and that I was ready for help. I was immediately admitted to the Psyche unit. I had to recognize that I had to admit, not only to myself but to my family, that I needed their help. I had to let go of my own pride and say YES. I praise God for on that day of January 15, 2002, my inner healing began. It was the beginning of my journey to a place of love that had been missing for so long. It was the beginning of me loving me. It was an experience I will never forget. I was afraid, but I wanted to live and not die. I had to let go of past behaviors and receive God's Love unconditionally. I had no idea what would happen in the hospital, but I knew I was trusting God because there was no other way. I knew nothing about mental illness, but at this point in my life, I was willing to try anything. I was in the hospital for two weeks and step by step, I arose out of the ashes and began to love on me. I thank God for every heartache and for every time I was misunderstood. I own my story and my actions. I am no longer a victim of my life and I am grateful that God put me in the care of a Christian Therapist, Dr. Ernest Webb, who taught me that healing truly comes through God; if I trust God with everything, my mind will be renewed to think only thoughts of peace and joy in any situation. I saw Dr. Webb faithfully every week for almost five years. Dr. Webb spoke life into me and especially the love of God to me. He refused to allow me to say anything negative and always brought my conversation back to my favorite scripture which is: "For I know the plans I have for you to prosper you. Plans to give you hope and a future (Jeremiah 29:11). My outlook on life has changed and I have never felt better and more whole in my whole life. I believe we all can be happy and live a fulfilled life no matter what your past is. I came from a life of alcohol, drugs, depression, and abuse and I now live a beautiful life. Most of all, I live a life of love. I have dropped my victim story and I have taken back my power and I am now in control of my life and my feelings. But it all began with self-love. We have a choice to select happiness or sadness, to choose mediocrity or excellence.

My prayer is that through my story, parents understand how important their role is in providing a secure loving foundation for their children.

> *It is important that parents listen, encourage, love, support and, invest seed of greatness within your children. Children must be supported emotionally, physically and academically. We are entrusted with these precious souls, and it is up to us as parents to protect and nurture them in the right environment. We must encourage children to speak about their feelings and not be afraid of being punished. We must have tough conversations with our family and friends. These are just some strategies that will give them a strong foundation that will allow them to grow into adults who have a positive impact on the world.*

I invite you to visit my blog at **www.be-an-intentional-parent.com** where I provide techniques to parents on becoming an intentional parent.

4

Life Hits Hard, But So Do I

Erika Gilchrist

Assaulted as a little girl, sleeping in a van as a young adult, and living in a women's shelter, Erika Gilchrist has earn the title of *"The Unstoppable Woman."* She is regarded as one of the most energizing, engaging, and captivating speakers in the industry.

She is the Producer & Host of W.T.F. – **W**omen **T**hriving **F**earlessly!, an online television talk show which showcases guests who share their stories of how to thrive. You can see past episodes at WomenThrivingFearlessly.com. Erika spends her life creating a global revolution of unstoppable women through her events which focuses on how to thrive fearlessly. As a published author of 9 books, she empowers entrepreneurs and professionals by teaching them how they can become published authors and position themselves as experts through the sharing of their stories. She guides women's groups through the process of creating collaborative books to generate revenue for their organization. She has a knack for bringing women together in a single space that breeds comradery, resourcefulness, and unique solutions for today's most challenging dilemmas. Ms. Gilchrist is an expert in personal development, book writing & self publishing, and conflict management. She's been featured as one of the *"15 Most Powerful Women on the South Side of Chicago,"* CLTV, and Rolling Out Magazine.

Erika Gilchrist
Award-Winning Speaker & Author
www.TheUnstoppableWoman.net
info@theunstoppablewoman.net
866-443-6769

> Here I stand on the other side of heartache, abuse, near-death experiences, and miraculous life twists to reveal what I've learned most about myself. Resiliency has been my strongest ally. See, you can't threaten someone with death who's not afraid to die – you can't shame a person for things of which they are not ashamed – and you can't stop someone who's unstoppable.

From the Beginning

At the tender age of 3, my daddy passed away in a tragic train accident while he was at work. At that time, it was my older sister, me, and a younger brother on the way. My sister and I went to live with my paternal grandmother who raised me. Our house was always too crowded for me. I didn't feel like I had any privacy, and it seemed as if there was always drama going on. I recall packing a bag and hiding it under my bed waiting for the right opportunity to run away. It wasn't all bad – just enough to drive me completely freaking insane on a regular basis.

When you grow up in a house full of people, one of two things happen as an adult. Either you crave a large family because you have grown accustomed to it, or you want nothing more than to be by yourself. I am the latter. Some of my best memories happened while I was alone.

I moved out when I was 19 years old, not knowing (or caring) what the world had in store for me. I just knew that I wanted to be on my own. I had NO IDEA how hard life would be. But it made me street smart, incredibly resourceful, and provided me with razor sharp intuition.

I also wasn't aware of how the death of my father impacted many of my decisions – particularly in my relationships with men. I was a chronic people pleaser and as a result, I ended up in relationships that did not serve me well. For those who know me today, it may come as a shock to learn that at one time, I was a complete pushover. Even if I found someone who I thought was compatible, I'd leave because I was terribly afraid of being abandoned. Being by myself was my default setting. I felt safe – nobody can leave me if I'm the only one around, right? I strongly suspect that I missed out on loving relationships because of my deeply rooted fear of abandonment.

But despite all of that, I've always had a sense that something about life was terribly "wrong." The things that were deemed as successful seemed ass backwards to me. Go to school, get a degree, get a "good" job, buy a house, raise a family, work for 40 years, and then retire. None of that appealed to me. In fact, I thought that process was like an invisible prison. Why the hell would anybody want THAT? But everywhere I looked, that's the message that was being conveyed. I felt like an alien on a planet that couldn't explain itself to me in a language that I would understand. With this internal rebellious need to "beat the machine," I set out to conquer the world. But instead, the world KICKED MY ASS.

Common American Scenario: Work your ass off five days a week, wait for the weekend to rest or celebrate, then rinse and repeat. For me? FUCK THAT.

The Little Rebel

I've known for quite some time that I was different. What I mean by that is simply that I recognized flaws in societal norms at a very early age. My first memory of this observation was when I was in the second grade and my teacher gave me bad marks for not doing my homework. She called my grandmother and told her that I was a very smart child, and in the classroom, I was well behaved. She just couldn't understand why I wouldn't do my homework. My grandmother confronted me about it and I did internal cartwheels because I was finally given the floor to express my confusion. I said, "I do the work in school over and over again, and I pass it. Why do I have to come home and do it again?"

That thought process continued throughout my adolescent years of education and in my freshman year of high school, the same scenario presented itself. This time, it was my Algebra teacher who called my grandmother. "She's a brilliant student; she's very well behaved, but I can't seem to get her to do any homework." Because I was older, I was able to better express myself. "I get straight A's in class, which proves that I have mastered the material. Explain to me why it's necessary for me to delay my extracurricular activities to accommodate the repetition of formulas for which I have no use?" I was 14.

I was never satisfied with the response, "Because that's the way it is," or, "It's always been done this way." That infuriated me because I kept thinking, "Then change it, damn! What's so hard about that? You see this isn't working, but you won't do anything about it." My life's pattern reveals that I seek out uncommon ways of achieving desirable results. Or as my multiple ex-boyfriends would say, "Doing shit the hard way."

Get Up!
I was about 21 years old when this situation occurred. I recall

that my car wasn't working, I had no money to get it repaired, I couldn't pay any bills, I was hungry, and I had no income coming in. I walked in the house feeling so incredibly defeated. I looked in the fridge to see that there wasn't much to eat, and then I looked through my cupboards and made the same observation. Then I looked in my medicine cabinet and saw a bottle of pills. I stood there, staring at the bottle, thinking about my life.

I poured myself a glass of tepid water, slid down the wall and sat in a corner of the room, and began taking the pills one at a time. With each pill, I thought of specific parts of my life. No money [PILL], no father [PILL], no career [PILL], I'm ugly [PILL], I'm worthless [PILL], I deserved to be abused [PILL], the world will be better off without me [PILL]...I began to sob uncontrollably for a long while and through my screams I heard something that startled me.

"Erika!" I whirled my head around to see who it was that called me. I was so startled that I spilled the water and dropped the rest of the pills. All of a sudden, I was terrified because I knew that I was supposed to be alone and I didn't want anyone to see me like this. My eyes darted back and forth around the room and I heard the voice again, "You're better than this. **GET UP!**" Because I was so scared, I obliged and scrambled to stand to my feet. But the moment that I stood completely erect, I no longer felt fear. I wanted to live! The room was spinning, I felt sleepy, and I entered a "twilight" state of consciousness, but somehow I was able to make it over to the sink to induce vomiting.

After my body heaved up as much of the pills and stomach acid as it could, I lifted my head from the sink and only one word came to mind: UNSTOPPABLE. And in that moment, "The Unstoppable Woman" was born.

I decided to seek professional help, and luckily I found a place that charged on a sliding scale. I paid $15 per session and for the next couple of years, I worked out many issues that were long overdue. What I discovered during that time set me on a path to self empowerment:

- The childhood abuse wasn't my fault
- Don't over romanticize relationships
- Saying "no" is acceptable and healthy
- I am beautiful...just as I am
- Shame can't hold you hostage when you've already freed yourself from it
- Confirmation: I enjoy being alone, and it's okay
- The best way out is through it
- Listen to the pain of others, not necessarily their words
- I am worthy of love

Slowly, I began to stand up for myself, set boundaries, and listen to my instincts. Another pattern in my life that developed was not to question _why_ many occurrences take place which [at the time] make no sense. I've learned that the purpose gets disclosed later in your life. I'll explain...

Tornados

I've always been fascinated by weather and the cosmos – changes in the atmosphere, our solar system, and the vastness of the Universe. I was drawn to stories in the media and documentaries regarding rescue efforts and how to survive natural disasters. Nothing in my life thus far was a direct connection to my obsession of these stories. But all of that changed in the summer of 1997.

I lived in Romulus, Michigan at the time – a suburb of Detroit. One day, I was traveling with my then boyfriend in his shiny new truck, and his 4 year old son in the back seat. My boyfriend, Quincy*, was very selfish when it came to his prized new truck. He refused to let me drive it even though I was allowed to drive his previous "not so new" vehicle. So often times I was frustrated because I hated the way he drove.

I don't recall exactly where we were going, but I do remember that in a matter of minutes, the skies went from partly sunny to gray - then to a darker shade of gray – then to damn near black. The wind picked up dramatically and it started to rain heavily. Then came the hail. I had watched enough of the weather channel to know exactly what that means. I strongly urged Quincy to pull over so we could wait out the storm inside of a building. I chose my words carefully because I didn't know how he'd respond to what I really wanted to say, "There's a fucking tornado coming! Pull yo ass over fool!" It seemed that my words fell on deaf ears, and he kept driving. Then I noticed trees toppling over, some of the buildings lost power, and the only light we had came from the momentary flashes of lightning. What we could clearly see were the power lines snapping because of the sparks. I continued to scream - begging him to pull over, and he refused. I didn't know from which direction the tornado was coming, and it sent me into a panic. My heart was pounding, my mind was racing, and my instinct kicked in and said, "Erika, get your ass the fuck outta here NOW NOW NOW!!!"

I wasted no more time. I disengaged my seatbelt, opened the door as wide as I could against the wind and jumped out of a moving vehicle. I'm glad he had sense enough to hit the brakes as I opened the damn door. When I swung my feet to jump out, a quick flash of lightning lit my path to a nearby restaurant. The timing of that flash was pure divinity – otherwise I'd literally be running aimlessly in near blackness. I entered the building and immediately noticed that there weren't any employees or patrons inside. I jumped over the counter and ran towards the back of the kitchen where I saw a door that was ajar. I entered the door and I could hear commotion from people and I instantly felt a wave of relief because I wasn't alone. Another flash of lightning vaguely revealed stairs in front of me – again, pure divinity kept me from falling down a flight of stairs. When I reached the bottom, I could see a group of people huddled together on the floor and one person was holding a flashlight. I joined them in the huddle and we all squeezed each other as hard as we could as we listened to glass breaking, screaming people, and unrecognizable destruction.

I'm sure it was just a couple of minutes that passed, but it certainly seemed like an eternity. When the tornado passed by, we lifted our heads slowly and began to assess ourselves to see if we'd been injured. Once I confirmed that I was physically okay, I looked around the room to see if anyone needed medical attention – I was a flight attendant at the time, and it was my training. When I glanced around, I inhaled deeply with my hands over my heart and mouth because I saw Quincy there on the floor with us, clutching his son to his chest.

I opened my mouth to ask him a question and as if he knew what I was going to ask he responded, "When you jumped out, I knew it was serious. I grabbed Quincy Jr.* and followed you inside." I looked down at his son's little face – wet, dirty, and frightened – and hugged him tightly until he stopped crying.

The years of learning what to do when tornadoes hit saved my life. At the time, I just found it fascinating. I never dreamed that I'd be faced with taking cover to protect myself from a deadly twister, especially since I lived in a heavily populated city with tall buildings.

Often times, we're faced with split second decisions that could literally mean the difference between life and death. If I chose to stay in the vehicle, ignoring my instincts, I'm sure the outcome would have been devastating for all three of us. Quincy knew that I had great instincts – we've had that conversation before. Why he deliberately chose to ignore my verbal commands during those

> *"Don't sink with the ship if you know how to swim."*
>
> – Erika Gilchrist

crucial moments, I don't know. But it took my _actions_ to get through to him, not my words. And because of that, he and his precious little boy were saved.

In the beginning of this chapter you read, "...you can't threaten someone with death who's not afraid to die..." Allow me to explain exactly when my fear of death dissipated.

Wings on the Way Down
Back in the early 2000's, I worked on construction sites as a union laborer. Yes, I know it may be difficult to picture me in a hard hat, overalls, and steel toed boots, but I did it and ROCKED at it. Now picture something else – An elevator with 8 people surrounding a large trash can full of drywall and tools. As the elevator climbed towards the 19th floor, we noticed that it began to slow down around the 15th floor. Naturally we assumed that someone called the elevator to get on so it wasn't a big deal. And then it happened...

It crept up to the 17th floor. After dangling in a manner that can only be described as bouncing, it suddenly began to plummet fiercely towards the basement. I recall my feet leaving the floor momentarily as I grabbed a strong hold of the trash can for support. I heard nothing but the sounds of air whooshing and the screams of the men and women who were with me trapped in a steel box falling from above.

I'm unclear about how many seconds we were falling, but I am crystal clear about the feeling itself. I found myself transitioning to a state of "letting go." I let go of the "what ifs" – what if I die? What if I get seriously injured? What if I never see my family again? At that time, everything seemed to be moving in slow motion. I could no longer hear anything as I glanced around to see the expressions of horror and shear panic on the faces of my team. It was like something straight out of a movie.

I looked up at the panel that indicates which floor you're passing, and the number "3" was illuminated. I smiled and thought, "Oh well. It's been a fun life." Then suddenly the elevator slowed down in the same manner as when you're driving in a car and slam on the brakes. We all were hurled towards the floor from the discontinued momentum of the fall and suddenly it felt like we hit a big pillow and the "Kssss" sound of the emergency brake filled the steel box. Scared and panicked, they nearly trampled me trying to exit when the doors opened. Thanks to the emergency brake, I lived to be a woman who thrives fearlessly.

But something else happened to me during that fall. I went from feeling scared to sacred – fearful to fearless – anxious to angelic. In the blink of an eye I actually EXPERIENCED the  separation of my human self and my spiritual self. I became an observer, not a participant. From that moment forward I no longer feared death, which freed me in a way that is indescribable. I often refer to that experience as the day when "I got my wings on the way down."

Deadly Game of Chicken

In my early 30's, I found myself in a second abusive relationship and one of the most physical occurrences happened one afternoon when we were alone in the house. I don't recall what the fight was about, but it ended with him shoving me against the wall, with his hands tightly wrapped around my throat.

Because of my first abusive relationship, I decided to take self defense classes. I learned how to crush an esophagus, break fingers, and how to counter attack. Bad news for this punk.

As he squeezed my neck harder, I just stared into his eyes, not flinching one bit. After a few seconds, I saw his facial expression change to one of pure confusion. Like he asked himself, "Why isn't she scared?" When I'd had enough (and I realized that it was hard to breathe), I initiated the counter attack and began to slowly crush his esophagus with my thumbs, smiling. It was like a sick game of chicken to see who would let go first. He released his grip and I started hoarsely laughing. I'm sure he thought that I was a psychopath ☺. I added, "If it ever comes down to one of our lives ending, I promise it'll be yours." Talk about feeling empowered! I felt as if I had made up for all the times when I didn't stand up for myself. Just like I learned in therapy, I am worthy of love – and **that** wasn't it.

"Me too!"

For a long time, it was very difficult to openly discuss my life experiences. I was embarrassed and ashamed. I didn't want people to treat me differently. I didn't want that stigma of victimhood following me everywhere I went. But I remembered what I learned in therapy – you can't be shamed for things that you expose on your own terms.

I began to speak publicly about my life on a very real and vulnerable level, and the results were beyond my wildest dreams. I started to get women approaching me after a speech with tears in their eyes and whisper the words, "Me too! Thank you!" That motivated me to continue, so I started revealing more details and the more I revealed, the stronger and more frequent the feedback became. The below is still one of the most heartfelt letters that I have received to date. It's from a woman in the UK who explained how she felt after reading one of my books:

> *"...the last thing I expected to do was to change my mind about killing myself. You, quite literally my dear, saved my life. My daughter thanks you, my mum thanks you, and I thank you!"*

How on earth can I stop empowering women after that?! I can't. It's what I'll do until I return to the cosmos. The healing of our hearts come when we share our stories with the world. You're not alone, you're not worthless, you're not irrelevant, and you're not undesirable. You are fierce, you are strong, you are influential, and you are a THRIVER!

The Checklist

For all intents and purposes, I should be a basket case if we examined the traditional outcomes of someone who has experienced the life issues that I had:

> ➢ Abandonment issues? [CHECK]
> ➢ Boughts of depression? [CHECK]
> ➢ Sexual abuse? [CHECK]
> ➢ Domestic violence? [CHECK]
> ➢ Extreme poverty? [CHECK]
> ➢ Homelessness? [CHECK]
> ➢ Body image issues? [CHECK]
> ➢ Self deprecating thoughts? [CHECK]

But I created another list. One that reflects the end result of getting through my most challenging life experiences:

> ➢ Ownership of choices [CHECK]
> ➢ Self love [CHECK]
> ➢ Successful in business [CHECK]
> ➢ Loving relationships [CHECK]
> ➢ Healthy body [CHECK]
> ➢ Tranquil home [CHECK]
> ➢ Emotional well being [CHECK]
> ➢ Mental stability [CHECK]
> ➢ True to myself [**DOUBLE** CHECK]

THIS is what it truly means to thrive fearlessly! I may still get blindsided from time to time and experience setbacks, which is expected. But when this happens, I have a purse full of devices designed to knock them on their ass.

So how do YOU thrive? In what ways have you gone from victim to vicTOR? Share that story! No more hiding. It's how we grow as individuals as well as a society. If you want my assistance in helping you to get your story out, and your voice heard, then reach out to me. Let's celebrate your journey together!

5

How You Do Anything is How You Do Everything

Lonnetta M. Albright

 Lonnetta Albright is one of the most dynamic and transformative speakers, facilitators and coaches working nationally and internationally adding value to and changing the lives of thousands. She is particularly focused on developing those she fondly calls the Next Generation. As President and Owner of Forward Movement Inc., a small minority and female owned company, she offers coaching for individuals and organizations, personal and professional growth, organizational and leadership development, speaking and consulting. As a certified personal and executive coach, she is a member of the John Maxwell Global Leadership Team. For the past 17 years, Lonnetta has served as Executive Director of the Great Lakes Addiction Technology Transfer Center/University of Illinois/Jane Addams College of Social Work. As a life-long learner who understands the value in "growing self first," her interest in positive psychology, human behavior, strength-based approaches, behavioral and public health, and the science that supports them all has not only increased her own understanding, but means her clients and audiences experience meaningful and real changes that shift their mindsets and behavior in ways that can be applied immediately. She is clear that her passion is working with and growing new leaders, new thinkers, and also women to help them to find their way, face their fears, and transform their lives. Her approaches and strategies are not just about personal and professional development – she helps her clients get results! Her popular "Heart-Mind-Time (HMT) program has impacted countless lives!

www.LonnettaAlbright.com
www.JohnMaxwellGroup.com/LonnettaAlbright
coach@lonnettaalbright.com
708-608-0364

> *"Much of my adult life was focused on saving people. I turned the mirror around and realized the person who needed to be saved was me."*

Because I said so!

Why was my mother's favorite answer, "Because I said so?" I wanted to challenge it; afraid to question her, I accepted it as the way to do anything.

It all fell apart when I was 19 years old - mama died. I was the oldest of four. I had 2 sisters and a baby brother who was more than a decade younger than me. Mom died on his birthday. Before she left us she asked me for the big promise – *"Will you help your dad with your sisters and help raise your brother?"* Of course, I said yes. She didn't know all I wanted to do was be like "her" even though I didn't know or understand her. What was her life's purpose? What was her journey? What made her unique? And why was her "go to" answer *because I said so?*

How was I to help my siblings in their grief when I was numb? If they asked for advice or needed guidance (especially my little brother), what would I say? And God help me when it came to making decisions. "Because I said so" was not going to fly with them.

As I got older I came to hate that answer. So many missed opportunities for learning *how to* make decisions. *Because I said so* didn't shine a light on why was she saying so. Did she consider implications, consequences, and risks? Were values or fear involved? Or did she simply have a strong connection to the belief *children were meant to be seen and not heard*? LOL. Maybe if she'd lived longer than 47 years, those answers would have been revealed.

But wait! Is this all true, or was this my need to blame or run away from what she did teach me? After all, she taught me about God, stressed the importance of being an independent thinker, taught me how to drive, advocated and helped pay for me to go away to college. And whenever she had to be away, I was given "big sister" responsibilities. But I still didn't know who I was or what I wanted. All I knew was I wanted to have her approval and to be a "good girl." I did what she told me to, including staying a virgin until marriage (because she said so). Well at least I did as long as she was living. Another story for another time.

Because I said so had such an effect on me. Four simple words allowed me to hide, to not think for myself, to seek approval from others, and since I'm being honest here, allowed me to lie. It was impossible for me to be "her." As much as I adored her, trusted her, and depended on her, it was time for me to grow up and stop pretending. Maybe that's why God took her.

The "Pretender"

People thought I was smart, brave, mature, and successful, but I was pretending, afraid of most things. As a young girl I got good grades, was a good student, good friend, good daughter, and a good sister. But I was scared. My report card included excellent grades; it was not the case with conduct. The box "Talks Too Much" was always checked. Mom even bought me a *Chatty Cathy* doll.

So why did I talk so much? Was it fear, was I trying to convince others I was good enough, brave enough, tall enough? I grew up small. My siblings and most of my friends were taller than me. I couldn't fight my way out of a paper bag. But I could talk my way "in and out of things," dad would say. They even thought I would be an attorney.

Still I was pretending, hiding behind my words, my strong critical thinking, and deductive and strategic abilities. My sisters will tell you I would talk a good talk, then they would have to step in and fight my physical battles - all true. They did, God bless them for it. Who knows where I would be without those two fearless girls who are now amazing women. But back to me. I was *Chicken Little* with a lot of mouth. I was afraid of water. My high school swim instructor got tired of me and pushed me in. I begged her not to, but she pushed and I pulled her in with me. My very first "F." I was afraid of worms, nature, darkness, and taking risks. I took caution to new heights. Not realizing in so doing, I was stunting my own development all in the name of safety. I guess talking helped me keep up my pretense.

My mother gave me an opportunity to pretend. It was my little brother - I could "pretend" to be a mom. Even though pretending, I was able to practice courage and love. He was still young enough, curious enough, needy but yet brave enough to challenge me and to ask "why?" He was smart too (it's in the genes). He wouldn't let me get away with *Because I Said So.* For both our sakes, I began to ask myself and taught him that we need to know our values, what it is we believe about ourselves, and how to go after what we wanted no matter what others' thought. As Deepak Chopra says, "Love is what we're born with, Fear is what we learn."

I carried "fake" Lonnetta into my relationships and my career. I got divorced blaming my ex and never once, from beginning through end, did I ask if marriage was what I wanted. What I did want, however, was to have sex and not be judged morally. No fornication!!! I figured if I married, I'd honor mom's rule (no sex before marriage), and daddy would stop raising his eyebrows, huffing and puffing whenever I'd stay out all night. This pretending thing was stifling me and any chance at a healthy and honest relationship.

I thought I had learned from my relationship mistakes, understood men, moved past my past, and healed from the hurt (particularly my divorce), without being bitter. Never mind I didn't ask transformative questions such as, *"What do I want? Am I worthy? What's my why? What does God intend for my life?"*

In my 30s it seemed the relationship I was in was a good one. My boyfriend wasn't like previous men who I'd tried to change or save. If I would have turned the mirror around, I would've seen that I was the one who needed to be saved and changed. *"The way I did anything is the way I did everything,"* especially in my intimate relationships.

My career path and accomplishments were a different story. While pretending in some ways, I was blessed with opportunities and mentors who helped me to "turn the mirror around."

There's no doubt in my mind that God's grace, patience and belief in me brought the right people and circumstances into my life. Still the pretending lingered. I wanted to be a kind and just manager. But opinions of others crept in – "Be assertive, tough, decisive, firm; don't make friends with those who you work with especially those who work for you." I took on a façade that was uncomfortable for me. I hated it. I told my dad, "I didn't go to school to be a boss; I wanted to be a school teacher." Long story short, Dad, my first mentor, taught me the value of fairness, justice, and integrity – the fundamental values of a good leader. And if I embraced those values the people and relationship part would follow.

At 37 my maternal grandmother created a stir inside of me that challenged my "Boss" and "Success" notions. I'd told her about my great accomplishments, promotions, supervision responsibilities, first research project, my "alleged great relationship," etc. She listened, and told me how proud she was. One night, she awoke, called me to her bedside and whispered, *"You have such a sweet spirit."* WHAT!!! Sweet spirit? What about the accomplishments I shared with her? Didn't she hear me? What was I to do with my training & advice from others - "You are too nice, work hard, toughen up, be direct; *Let people know who's in charge."* So when Granny said that to me I exhaled. You mean it's okay to be kind and forgiving - to be me? She gave me permission to embrace my true essence, *"But the fruit of the Spirit is love, joy, peace, patience, kindness, goodness, faithfulness, gentleness and self-control. Against such things there is no law."* Galatians 5:22-23

A True Out of Body Experience

There was still much to do and learn. I hadn't figured out how to have a healthy, loving and honest relationship. So God stepped in and decided it was time for us to take a ride.

Just past dawn one Saturday, I was driving to my boyfriend's house. I didn't want to go but *"the way I did anything was the way I did everything"* – putting others first, placing what I wanted on the back burner. As I pulled up to a stop light, I looked over at the driver in the car next to me, and noticed a woman who, when

I smiled at her, had hurt, pain, and confusion in her eyes. I glanced back, just for a second; her face morphed into my face. My past mistakes and poor decisions flashed across my mind. I thought, "Wow! That could have been me! Maybe it is me." I wondered if others could look at me and see the pain, confusion, guilt  and unhappiness that was in my heart, possibly showing on my face. As I rushed through the green light, I peered in my rear view mirror to see if what I'd experienced was a mirage. I continued what was less than a mile long drive through a community where I'd hung out in various places. Nightclubs, bars, parks – everything looked gloomy and empty. I'd spent a year or two hanging out there because I dated a guy who "I wanted to save." Well I must have slipped into some type of dream state, or so it seemed. As I passed an empty lot, I could see a pack of pit bulls and one lone poodle. The poodle was me - not just my face, but I was actually the poodle. The leader of the pack came over to me with a murderous look, and teeth that could tear my small fluffy head off. He said, "*Silly little dog, we could kill you in a second; but you're so stupid for being out here I am going to let you go. So run - run for your life and never come back!*"

Still in a dream state, heart pounding, I began to pray. *God please forgive me for sins I've committed, mistakes I've made, for ignoring you and all my mother had taught me. Please forgive me.* That's when God spoke to me. I could literally hear Him. Not so much the burning bush sort of voice, but His voice for sure. "*Sweetheart don't you know, I forgave you long ago? It's time for you to forgive yourself. All those mistakes and the life you've been living is not what I've intended for you.*"

When I snapped out of it, I was sitting at a stop light, having driven maybe 6 blocks, but it felt as though I'd been there for an hour. I pulled over, tears rolling and a bit freaked out...actually a **lot** freaked out. My journey towards self-forgiveness would take a year or more.

Dumped

Of course I blamed my boyfriend. Of course he was wrong. Somewhere in my subconscious mind I knew I had played a role. I had shut out God, I shut out wisdom from my mom, and I talked my way around Dad. Don't forget, I had a future as an attorney. And as was my pattern, *the way I did anything, was the way I did everything* – seeking approval of others, pretending and "lying."

He was well-respected, highly regarded, and self-assured. Because I perceived him as different from previous guys, I thought, "This is it!" I'd go to fancy fundraisers, dress and look the part, say what was appropriate while all along I wanted to challenge what I'd hear. I wanted to call a "spade a spade" and not play politics. I remember one such event when I was dressed to the nines, a diamond (fake) on my finger and holding my own in conversation. I felt like a fraud. They were the elite, highly educated with big positions; they had arrived. I think they could see my distaste even though I tried to cover it up since after all, I had a big position too. Even to this day I cannot stand any type of separation between people (status, race, financial or otherwise). So why was it so difficult to stand my ground? I tried to share my beliefs and opinions but I still wasn't my own person. I was not yet comfortable in my own skin.

One evening, I got quiet and honest with myself saying out loud, "I can no longer make an agreement with what I don't want."

The relationship was not serving me well.   My fear and pretender roles needed to be conquered.

I knew that if I asked for what I wanted, the relationship could go either way. Well it didn't go as I thought I wanted it to. I was devastated, deflated and afraid of being alone. I couldn't talk my way around the pain and confusion. But I was also determined to feel the pain and come out on the other side. I entered therapy for the first time, and what a treat. To have someone whose only goal was to help me become the best version of myself was life changing.

While on my healing journey, I read a book called "Dumped" which was written by women from various walks of life. And there it was. I'd been dumped! I could name it, move on and deal with it. Still, I hadn't accepted my part in the break-up.

On my own it seemed the flood gates opened. What showed up in the form of rejection was actually freedom - *free at last, free at last, thank God almighty – Would the real Lonnetta please stand up?!!!* I don't remember the exact day or month, but questions I'd been holding at bay began to surface:

- How do I create a personal and intimate relationship with God if all I feel is tradition and ritual?
- Isn't it okay for me to go to the movies alone, sit in a bar and listen to music-alone, take a vacation-alone?
- Does success require that I win?
- Isn't it okay to lose?
- Do I talk too much?
- What's wrong with talking?
- What's wrong with being selfish?
- Isn't it okay to sacrifice for someone else?

- Why is kindness perceived as weakness?
- How will I set boundaries?
- What's the power in the word No?
- Why do I say yes when I mean No?
- What's wrong with being devoted to my family?
- Is it okay to not know something?
- What is it I want and what's my unique path?

Many of these are questions my coaching clients ask today. The great news is that answers are always within us. I found my answers deep within me. And they continue to come, I welcome them; I search for them and will continue to do so - that's my unique path, my right and I am worthy.

In my new "free & independent" life I began to blossom. I realized the connection between my "out of body experience" and being dumped. It's quite possible the pit bull encounter was a pivotal one, preparing me to run towards my uniqueness. So I now ask, "Is it possible that I 'dumped' myself?" Pretty cool, huh? And pretty self-aware.

What About My Life? Freedom & Transformation
The way you do anything, is the way you do everything – until you make the subconscious conscious. For the last 10 years I've spent time getting out of my head and into my heart. I call it my Next Chapter and **I am doing everything differently**.

I reflect on a day I spent with my nephew when he was a toddler. He'd wanted to hang out with me one Saturday, and it unfolded something like this:

ME: *You can come along if you'd like, but I have lots of errands.*

HIM: *Okay, I still want to go.*

After about 2 hours, he had his own ideas and interests.

HIM: *When are we going to do something I want to do?*
ME: *Don't you remember, you agreed to come along while I run my errands?*
HIM: *Yeah, I remember, but what about my life?*

It was a simple but profound question that has served me well as I continued to grow and develop. Whenever I slip, attempt to get someone's approval, or give them what they want, I ask myself, "What about *my* life?"

With God, therapy, coaching, mentors, friends, and my amazing family, I found the truth of me. I discovered that to have a deep and intimate relationship with God requires spirituality, which is much different from religion. And yes, I got good at taking risks, making mistakes, and seeing them as new opportunities. It wasn't easy; it took a while and I keep growing. Another lesson that I hope is coming through loud and clear here – *we must grow ourselves first if we want to grow others.* So I ask, "Do you have a personal growth plan?"

And that thing about being dumped, I came out on the other side able to forgive, and to see what part I played. I saw the good things that came from the relationship such as my love for travel, exposing myself to new things, spending time alone and enjoying my own company. I know what movies I like. I go alone when no one wants to see what I want to see. I travel alone when no one wants to go where I want to go (Jamaica at the top of my list). I try new things, meet all kinds of wonderful people, dance as often as I can, and no longer pretend or seek approval. Yes, I'd lost someone else, but gained a life – my uniqueness.

My past is gone. I cherish and use the great things that serve me well such as my mom's favorite scripture, Proverbs 3:6 *"In all your ways acknowledge God and He will direct your path..* So I started to do just that. I don't always get it right nor do I check in with him always. When I don't, things can get a bit murky. When I do, activation happens. My dad also helped me to activate my intentions, "Know thyself and always do the right thing."

> *My siblings taught me "you are not alone" and just because I was the oldest didn't mean I had to have all the answers. Nor did it mean I was the leader if when I turned around they were going in the other direction. As for the rest of my past, all is forgiven and <u>forgotten</u>.*

So what about my life? Every day unfolds the next step in my journey. Faith has taught me to take the first step even when I can't see the entire staircase. While I believe Love is the greatest commandment, it doesn't mean putting everyone else before me, what I want, or the type of person I want to be or be with.

My 1st chapter, has been a successful one - a stellar career, world travel, tremendous relationships and networks. I've made a difference in many lives. I want to do more, requiring me to engage my own Life Coach.

My 2nd chapter is a big dream. I now know I can do, have and be whatever I want in all areas of my life. So can you. It's not easy but it's fun. You don't need others' approval. They have their unique journey, their "Why" as do you and I.

My "Why" is to live a life of significance, adding value to others. That's my intent here in this chapter. For baby boomers such as myself, please believe it's never too late to live your dreams. And to our next generation, start dreaming now; listen to and follow your dreams. Dream Big!!!! And yes, we can learn to forgive and **forget.**

It's no accident I share this journey with you, nor is it a surprise. It's my choice and my purpose. As I stretch beyond my comfort zone I do so with God's presence every step of the way. #Faith

6

Advocate for Me

L'Vonne McMillan

L'Vonne McMillan has worked with various agencies providing one-on-one instruction and early intervention with clients with various special needs - Autism, Down Syndrome, and Mental Health Disorders. She has a wide range of experience in the Social Services Field as well as Lead Classroom Teacher at various locations. She started providing tutoring services in June 2004, and has had many families utilize her services with the following subjects: General Mathematics, Algebra, Geometry, Reading, and Writing. With this passion, she started the Marie Morgan Educational Center, Inc. The business was placed on hold due to her son's health. Now that Jordan's health is maintained at a better level, she is able to continue with her passion in working with women and children. She is embarking on a future business with a partner to open a teen pregnancy group home. Ms. McMillan's goal is to enhance the lives of others and to make their life more self sufficient with the gifts and talents that have been bestowed upon her as an Educator, Speaker, Dancer, Social Services Worker and now Co-Author. Her mission and purpose is to advocate for others.   L'Vonne shares this experience with her two children, family, and friends. Her driving force is providing her children with self sufficiency and to give them the best that she possibly can as a mother.

Email: mariemorganctr2@gmail.com
Facebook: www.facebook.com/mmec04

> ## My Life Line
>
> *"The bond between a girl and her grandmother is one that is deeply rooted in the shaping of her young adult years, and it keeps you grounded in times of turbulence. But what I didn't know is that that can all change...very suddenly.*

My grandmother became ill as I prepared to go to my cousin's High School graduation. My uncle, aunt, and I were driving to Virginia for the graduation. I called my aunt to take my grandma to the hospital because she was not feeling well for a few days. When we returned to Philadelphia, PA, I called home and was informed that my grandma was not doing very well, so my uncle drove me home instead of going to their house. He stopped at a gas station and I had a vision of my grandmother.

In the vision, I was at the bedside of my grandma. We had a conversation and she was saying how proud of me she was and to continue to do a great job. I told her I loved her and gave her a kiss. She smiled and we held hands. Just then, my Uncle jumped in the car and he pulled off. We turned the corner to my house. My heart started pounding again. As I put my key in the door and turned the knob, the phone rang inside the house. My mom began to scream a piercing scream and I knew what that phone call was about. She said, "The doctor said that mommy just passed away." I screamed, "Grandma, I am here! You couldn't wait for me to say goodbye." I sat down in the street and cried. My family brought me back into the house where I just laid on the bed numb. The pain hurt so much because I was angry with myself for sending her to the hospital, then I was angry with myself because I wasn't there for her when she needed me. I was not there for the woman who prayed for me when I was born a premature baby. My grandma - the one who taught me to get a valuable education, and reach for the stars. The woman who I cared for daily was gone. She left me; my lifeline was gone on June 16, 1995 around 11:36PM.

You are my sunshine

In January 2007, I was told I was pregnant with my first child. I was so scared. I had just turned 30 years old on January 3rd and on January 17th I was told I was going to be a mother. As time went on, I wondered what my child would look like. I had to wait until September to see. Everyone was getting ready for Memorial Day weekend. I was not feeling it. It was hot and I wanted to go to sleep. On Friday night, I was lying in the bed and my favorite car commercial came on the TV. The commercial has the song, "You are my sunshine." Every time the commercial came on I began to cry, rub my stomach and sang:

You are my sunshine, my only sunshine
You make me happy when skies are gray
You'll never know dear, how much I love you
Please don't take my sunshine away[1]

After I finished watching the show I turned the TV off and went to bed. I woke up a few hours later to go to the bathroom and I noticed blood. I called my boyfriend and went upstairs to get my mom. We walked to the hospital about 10 blocks away from my house, and when I arrived to emergency room they sent us to labor and delivery. I was seen by the doctor and was told that I was in labor but I was not dilated. The doctor said that I was to be on bed rest for the rest of the weekend and to see my prenatal physician at my scheduled appointment. So I was in the house all weekend. While everyone left me to go to barbeques I just slept. My back was hurting really bad but there was no more bleeding.

I returned to work and followed up with my prenatal care doctor and she said everything was fine. I scheduled my sugar test and my next appointment. Everything seemed to be fine, but I was really tired. One day at work I was having back pains really bad so I finished my day and went home. I called off the next morning because the pain was really bad. I was home by myself while everyone went to work and school. I slept and moaned because the pain was unbearable.

Late at night around 2am, I had to go to the bathroom, and as I picked my legs up to swing them out the bed I heard something pop. I ran to the toilet and began to pee but after a few minutes I was still peeing. I asked my brother to get my mom. I told her what happened and she was still dazed from her sleep. She said, "Just sit there, you will be finish soon." She walked away to return to her room and she ran back and said, "Your water broke!" I said, "No, it didn't I'm not due until September." My brother and my mom called the ambulance and my boyfriend. The operator told my brother to have me lay on my side while I wait for the paramedics to come. As I rose from the toilet, water was still running. I looked in the mirror and I said, "Oh no, my hair is all over my head. It looks a mess, I need a scarf." As I ran around looking for a scarf for my head, my brother was chasing me and telling me to lie down on my side. I found a scarf and lay down. I was so nervous I did not know what was going on. "Am I losing my baby? Is he okay? Did I work too much or did I return to work too soon?" The paramedics arrived and I didn't know what to do. They placed me on a stretcher and gave me a towel for the leaking. My mom went in the ambulance with me. The paramedic asked me a million questions: Name? Age? Birthdate? Insurance? It dawned on me what the date was - June 16. I really began to get nervous, Lord are you taking my baby too?

We arrived at the emergency room and the nurses were at the entrance with a wheelchair. They asked me to stand up and sit in the wheelchair. The paramedic helped me to get out of the ambulance, and as I raised my foot to step down I heard another pop and a gush of water like a waterfall came rushing out of my body. The paramedic screamed, "Whoa whoa! Okay sit down in the chair so we can get you upstairs to labor and delivery." When we arrived to the labor and delivery room the nurse asked me to walk to the counter to register. I stood up and I heard my mom scream, "Blood! Look she is bleeding!"I turned around to ask where and I felt another pop. This time it was not water. It was a glob of blood on the floor. The nurse ran over and they rushed me to the room. The doctor and nurse were giving me an examination and the doctor stated, "I am unable to see - it is so much blood." She ordered the nurse to turn on the heart beat monitor. As she turned it on my heart stopped. "Please God let my baby be okay." A few seconds passed, but it felt like an eternity and then there was a heartbeat. The nurse turned up the monitor and stated that the baby had a strong heartbeat. The doctors and nurses cleaned me off and removed me from the machines. The doctor ordered a shot that would help the baby's lungs grow quicker because he is going to be born soon due to my water breaking. They wheeled me to a room and put me on more monitors. The doctor said, "Get some rest, it's going to be a long day."

The nurse came into the room later that night but this time she was walking fast. She said, "Could you turn on your side?" I did. She looked worried and went back out the room. She walked out the room and then came back and asked me to turn on my other side. She walked quickly out the room, but this time when she came back she had like 10 doctors and nurses with her. They had another stretcher and asked me to get on the stretcher but to sit up on my hands and knees. The other doctor looked at my boyfriend who was startled out of his sleep. He asked him if he was the father, and my boyfriend said yes. Then the doctor said, "Come with me." The staff wheeled me down the hospital hallway on the stretcher while I laid on it doggie style (hands and knees on the bed). The cool wind of them pushing the bed so fast was rushing across my back. We went into two big doors and they asked me to lie down on my back. Just then my body began to shake uncontrollably. The nurse asked me if I was cold and I said yes, and he put a heat lamp and two warm blankets on me. But I continued to shake. I had an emergency C-section and at 11:36PM on June 16, 2007 my son- Jordan Smith was born. How could God pick the day that I lost a special person to be my son's birthday?

101 days

That day I slept all day long - the experience had taken a toll on my body. Prior to this, I never had surgery or been in a hospital overnight except when I was born prematurely myself at 2lbs 2oz. This day began my journey of my experience with my son. As soon as the pain medication wore off, my first question was, "Where is my baby?" The nurse went out to page the doctor and the doctor came in to tell me what happened during labor and delivery. She told me that my water broke due to an unforeseen reason. It could have been an infection that caused my body to react and give birth. Because of this, they had to get the baby out of the womb as quickly as possible. Because the baby's heartbeat was slowing, he went into distress. The doctors also explained that they placed me on antibiotics to fight the infection as well as pain medication due to the surgery. So I looked at the doctor and asked again, "Where is my baby?" The doctor explained that he was born prematurely and is very sick, but he is in the Neo-natal intensive care unit (NICU) of the University of Pennsylvania

Hospital. He will be there until he is better. How could this happen to a person who doesn't smoke, do drugs, or drink during my pregnancy?

The next morning, I was in so much pain from the stitches, but all I thought about was going to see my son in NICU. I awoke to the nurse coming in to do her rounds and I told her that I wanted to see my baby. She said that she would see what she could do and schedule for a wheelchair to take me to the NICU later that day. Later on that day, the orderly arrived with a wheelchair to take me to the NICU. As the orderly pushed me into the room of crying babies and monitors beeping, my heart began to pound. As we turned the corner of the room, there he was, Baby McMillan, lying in an incubator with lots of monitors and tubes connected to him. My heart sank, "My baby..." I said as I touched the glass of the incubator with tears rolling down my face. His Pediatrician came over with a box of tissues. She explained to me that my son was very sick and that he needs a lot of attention and care. I asked when he could come home and she said that he would be at the hospital for a long time.

The next four days while I was in the hospital I got up, I got dressed, I ate breakfast, and then I sat at my baby's bedside from 8am-11pm. The nurses would encourage me to talk to him so he can recognize my voice. From that day forward I would come to the NICU, greet the staff, read and sing to him. The songs I would sing to him were, "This little light of mine," "You are my sunshine," and "I know it was the blood." After a few weeks passed, Jordan had 1 blood transfusion, he was doing well, and he was breathing on his own. His eyes were fully developed so they removed the mask from his eyes. His skin was filling in and I no longer saw his tiny green veins through his skin. He was starting to move around, and his cry was getting stronger. I remember when I was able to hold him for the first time. Prior to this day I would put my hand in the incubator where there was a little circle door and I would rub his foot and sang the songs. This particular day the nurse asked if I wanted to hold him and I said yes. She explained to me that in the NICU, babies are so small that they are held close to their mother's chest and they need warmth. She took my son out of the incubator and put him in my shirt. I was so scared to hold him because he was so little but the moment we touched skin to skin all my worries was gone. I finally got to hold my baby. Every day I was there, even when I had to walk from my house to the hospital still in pain from the C-section. But nothing would keep me from my son.

After seeing him one day I went home to get some rest. I cried and cried I couldn't understand why God chose me to go through this. All my friends and family who had healthy babies got to bring home their babies and were enjoying motherhood. Why did I have to go through this and have my baby suffer? It is now a few weeks later and I inquired about the notice of birth so I can go get his social security card. The social worker came to Jordan's bedside where we discussed the paperwork procedures and how to get the social security card. The social worker informed me that he was not sure if they could release the notice of birth because Jordan was so sick that they were not sure if he would make it. I asked the social worker to repeat what he said and as calmly but as sternly as I knew how. I told the social worker, "I am not sure who you serve, but the God that I serve tells me that my son will live and that he will be just fine. So if you kindly give me his papers." The social worker gave me Jordan's paperwork and I proceeded to get Jordan's birth documents in order. Jordan had great doctors and nurses; they cared for him very well. I noticed some babies in the NICU who did not have any relatives visit them at all. I wondered how you could have your baby sit in here without seeing them or holding them. We had a long battle with Jordan's health from Cardiologists, Sugar tests, heart conditions, eye doctors, and medications such as water pills, caffeine pills, blood pressure medicine, 3 blood transfusions, and a host of other issues. Jordan was a tough cookie; he fought through most of his ordeals in the NICU and I was there every day except one. My baby shower was in August and I was gone all day after the shower. I went straight to the NICU and I was informed that he cried all day long, and the nurses couldn't console him. He just settled down to go to sleep. I knew that my being there on a day-to-day basis was helping him and encouraging him to get better. I never missed a day after that.

Jordan was discharged in September of 2007. He spent a total of 101 days in the NICU. I was so pleased to have him home but scared also. Our journey begins. Jordan came home with a breathing and heart monitor that would beep either of them reached below a certain number. The first three days he was home I could not go to sleep. I watched him all day and all night. I knew in the NICU he had round the clock care and at home, I was not a skilled nurse. His machine would beep and I would be right there tapping his feet to get him to wake up. I began to work at a residential group home during the night shift so I could be home for him during the day. Our journey began with multiple doctors' visits to the Cardiologist, Well Baby Check Up, Ophthalmologist, and Primary Pediatrician. After a visit with the Pediatrician she stated that Jordan should be emerging into sitting up on his own. She introduced me to a program that will assist with Early Intervention Services for children with special needs and disabilities. Jordan received Early Development Services through various agencies and he began to develop age appropriate skills by the therapist giving suggestions and activities to do with Jordan that would increase his developmental skills. Jordan received services until age 5. He was developing at his normal age level, but he still had some issues with feeding. As we went to various doctors we were sent to the allergy and asthma department where they informed us that Jordan has a rare condition called Eosinophilic esophagitis. It's a chronic allergic inflammatory disease of the esophagus. Today, Jordan is thriving developmentally; he is an honor roll student going to the 4th grade at GLA in Philadelphia, PA. Jordan is on a feeding tube and he is receiving care with his feeds on a daily basis by a nurse and at home. I loved watching my son grow from this tiny little baby, to this smart handsome young boy. I was his voice during this journey; I spoke for him when no one else could. I was his advocate.

Advocate for ME!

As the parent of a child with a special need or disability, I had to take the focus off of me and make my son my main priority.

I chose to leave numerous jobs to care for my son. One day his service coordinator came for a home visit and she stated that, "I would be good as a Service Coordinator." I took it into consideration but never pursued it until 2009. I really enjoyed working with the families and interacting with the children. I would often share my story with the parents just to ease the transition of their concern for their child and the new transition in life that they were about to experience - doctor's appointments, developmental pediatricians, therapists, early intervention, and tons of paperwork. I felt as though I was a beacon of light in their new phase of life. I would share with the families that as long as they work with the Early Childhood

Interventionist and use the suggestions that are provided by the therapists, they would see progress in their children - from outcome goals, to a thriving child that can accomplish their goals when they set their mind to it. As an advocate for your child, you are their voice. Is it going to be overwhelming? Yes! Are you going to have sleepless nights? Yes! Are you going to worry about your child's progress? Yes! Are you going to be there for your child? Yes! Some days are challenging. Sometimes I found myself overwhelmed by what the doctors were requesting, or the many times in the hospital with biopsy procedures, and changing feeding tubes. But at the end of the day, if I saw a smile on Jordan's face, or him resting peacefully and not in pain, then I knew I did my best. As a parent you should be thankful that God has placed a "SPECIAL" person in your life:

Special
Person
Experiencing
Childhood
In
Astonishing
Life

As their Advocate you have to see yourself as:
Adult
Doing
Valuable
Outstanding
Courageous
Actions
To have my child be
Exceptional

7

Transforming Pain to Power

Dr. Mimi D. Johnson

Dr. Mimi D. Johnson, "The Transformationalist," DMin, is an authentic, down-to-earth women's transformational expert, Certified Life Coach, Author, television and radio talk show Host, and gifted inspirational speaker. As the owner of MJM – (Mimi Johnson Motivations), an empowerment firm, she assures that her audience, mentees, and clients receive research proven, spiritually, and universally based principles and strategies which incorporate changing the way you think.

Affectionately known as Dr. Mimi, she has a dazzling smile, energetic presence, and sassy style that peaks the curiosity and attracts many to hear her speak at workshops, seminars, churches, and conferences. She has a passion for coaching women and helping them to discover their inner peace, harmony, and Divine nature for truth and fulfillment.

An Educator of Diverse Learners as well as an Ordained Minister, Dr. Mimi has a passion for Scripture, Bible stories, and sharing her message of "Living the Life that You Crave." After encouraging her mom to grow through her journey with breast cancer, Dr. Mimi became awakened to her purpose and passion in life. She overcame shame, guilt, depression, and multiple traumatic, life-altering events, after doing her own work. She is married to her amazing husband, David Sr., and has two awesome children, Quiana Joy and David Aidan, II.

Dr. Mimi understands what it means to move from "PAIN to POWER." She shows you how to use faith, belief in your ability, persistence, and determination to make your own transformation. She strongly believes that GOD is our Source and that his WORD is our GPS for today's living.

www.drmimijohnson.com
drmimij@sbcglobal.net
888-673-9012

BROKEN BEGINNINGS

Who would have ever known that a dysfunctional beginning - housing projects, molestation, guns, domestic violence, suicidal thoughts, and multiple traumatic experiences - would lead me to discover my Destiny as a Divinely Empowered Goddess?

BEGINNING OF SHAME

I recall my first home quite vividly.   There were 16 story buildings standing in clusters, gang and sexual graffiti scrawled upon large, cinder block walls (which gave a prison like feeling), hallway smells of urine, broken out windows, wintery busted pipes frozen with icicles, and lying in plain view of children were playgrounds sprawled with broken glass from alcohol bottles. I remember this scene as if it were yesterday.

The reason that I can tell you the clear memories of a four year old living in apartment 1107 of the 1847 W. Lake St. Henry Horner Housing Project, is because this is where "IT" occurred.

I would sometimes visit my Aunt Liz's apartment where my cousin JoAnn would babysit. I was allowed to walk alone up the stairwell three flights to apartment number 1402.

On this particular day, as I turned the corner in the stairwell heading up the next flight, "BOO", the building's known "mentally disabled" resident, happened to be sitting there alone in the stairwell. My four year old instincts began to kick in and told me that something was not right. I may not have known a whole lot at such a young age, but I knew for damn sure that someone sitting in a dark, stuffy, smelly, stairwell was absolutely insane.

Whenever we had to take the stairs because the elevator was down, (which turned out to be quite often), I walked through them as fast as I could because they always stunk and smelled like PISS! It was so strong that I would become nauseated and even gag.

He said, "Hi." I hesitated and reluctantly said, "Hi," as I tried to squeeze past his large body which took up most of the stair space. He blocked me from continuing upward by opening his legs wider to take up the remainder of the space. He continued to speak nicely to me so that I wouldn't notice what he was doing. He was using grooming tactics in order to relax me. I mumbled answers to his questions as he picked me up and sat me on his lap. I knew exactly what he was doing and I knew that I did not like the way this was making me feel. My stomach felt queasy and upset.

He continued to make small talk as he placed his hands on me, and began to touch and feel all over my body. I went inside my mind to escape. I thought about a story I had just read of an octopus with many arms moving quickly all over the place. He stuck his yucky tongue down my throat.

I just sat there with my mind racing. I didn't scream, I didn't cry. Maybe this was because he was speaking in a sweet tone, maybe this was because I "knew" him, or maybe this was because he wasn't "forcing" himself on me. He never threatened my family, he didn't yell or cuss, he didn't hurt me physically, nor did he swear me to secrecy. When he was done being pleasured, he simply stood me up and told me bye and that he would see me later.

For over forty years, I held this "BOO" secret AND shame, never telling a soul. This was my first traumatic childhood experience. This however, was only the beginning.

THE TRAUMA CONTINUES

In addition to the shame of being molested, these are brief highlights of the other traumatic events I experienced before I reached the age of eighteen.

GUILT and PAIN– The guilt that I lived with for over forty years as a five year old babysitting my four year old sister who suffered third degree burns while on my watch.

FEAR and PAIN - The fear that I lived with for over forty years as I witnessed infidelity and domestic violence in the relationship between my parents. I grew up with the feelings of insecurity, instability, and distrust.

SHAME, PAIN and FEAR- The shame that I lived with for over forty years from being shot at the age of eleven, as my parents fought over a handgun that went off.

FEAR – The fear that I lived with for close to forty years while working as a Burger King cashier. At the ages of sixteen and seventeen, I had a gun pointed in my face as I was robbed twice - two years in a row by the same unmasked man.

FEAR – The fear that I lived with for close to forty years after having a gun pointed at me at the age of seventeen and a half, for no apparent reason, by another young driver who pulled alongside me at a red light.

These happen to be the traumatic events that I experienced on my journey all before the age of 18. I allowed these traumatic childhood and teenage adverse experiences to keep me held hostage in fear, shame, guilt, and pain. They kept me from living a mentally and spiritually healthy and joyous life. They caused me to hold anger and bitterness, make poor choices, and dishonor myself.

I never told anyone how these experiences made me feel inside. Therapy and counseling was not accepted at that time as it is somewhat accepted today. To be honest, I never even knew that all of this unresolved trauma had such an effect on me and my family.

HEALING BEGINS

I began to seek spiritual guidance. I established an intimate relationship with my Creator by reading the Bible, feeding my Spirit with good ministry and spiritual programming day in and day out. I totally immersed myself in getting closer to God. I questioned, I sought, and I knocked. I began to develop a higher consciousness about my life and my connection to the great "I AM." Thus, began my healing journey.

I began to pour love from the Creator over myself. I looked up Scriptures that told me how my Father felt about me.

I affirmed (made positive statements) and declared what God says about me. I passionately repeated these words over myself morning, noon and night. I slowly began to BELIEVE, FEEL, and then KNOW that God loves me. I am so sure now that I know this in my very being, down into my core, down into my cellular level and DNA. God loves me JUST THE WAY I AM. He says that when he breathed life into my body that I AM GOOD! This is exactly what I tell myself!!

I have since learned that all of my experiences were planned before I was born so that I could learn the lessons, pass the testings, and receive the blessings by becoming the evolved person that I was intended to become for this life. I share my stories when I speak. As a transformational speaker, the Creator made sure that I would have stories of transformation to share!!!

I no longer ask, "Why did this happen to me?" I now say, "Thank you Creator for ALL of my experiences." It is in this that I have truly become a person who has learned to love myself, control my emotions, allow others to be themselves without judgment, how to think for myself, and to radiate love throughout the Universe. I remember as a child wanting my life to end. I am so grateful that God saw otherwise and graced me to be here at this time.

Adverse Childhood Experiences

In doing my healing research, I learned about Adverse Childhood Experiences, or ACEs, which are potentially traumatic childhood events that can have negative, long lasting effects. The ACE study shows that children who have had multiple traumatic experiences, go on to later have difficulties in their lives.

Adverse childhood experiences include:
• Emotional abuse
• Physical abuse
• Sexual abuse
• Emotional neglect
• Physical neglect
• Mother treated violently
• Household substance abuse
• Household mental illness
• Parental separation or divorce
• Incarcerated household member

A 1998 study from the Centers for Disease Control and

Prevention (CDC) and Kaiser Permanente is leading to a paradigm shift in the medical community's approach to disease. This study of more than 17,000 middle-class Americans documented quite clearly that adverse childhood experiences (ACEs) can contribute significantly to negative adult physical and mental health outcomes and affect more than 60% of adults. This continues to be reaffirmed with more recent studies.

While some stress in life is normal—and even necessary for development—the type of stress that results when a child experiences ACEs may become toxic when there is "strong, frequent, or prolonged activation of the body's stress response systems in the absence of the buffering protection of a supportive, adult relationship."

The biological response to this toxic stress can be incredibly destructive and last a lifetime. Researchers have found many of the most common adult life-threatening health conditions, including obesity, heart disease, alcoholism, and drug use, are directly related to childhood adversity. A child who has experienced ACEs is more likely to have learning and behavioral issues and is at higher risk for early initiation of sexual activity and adolescent pregnancy. These effects can be magnified through generations if the traumatic experiences are not addressed.

What happens in different stages of life is influenced by the events and experiences that precede it and can influence health over the life span. Importantly, an extensive body of research now exists demonstrating the effect of traumatic stress on brain development. Healthy brain development can be disrupted or impaired by prolonged, pathologic stress response with significant and lifelong implications for learning, behavior, health, and adult functioning.

A child needs to experience some emotional stress to develop healthy coping mechanisms and problem-solving skills. Experts categorize stress as: *"positive, helping to guide growth; tolerable, which, while not helpful, will cause no permanent damage; or toxic, which is sufficient to overcome the child's undeveloped coping mechanisms and lead to long-term impairment and illness."*

Toxic stress response can occur when a child experiences strong, frequent, or prolonged adversity, such as physical or emotional abuse, chronic neglect, caregiver substance abuse or mental illness, exposure to violence, or the accumulated burdens of family economic hardship, in the absence of adequate adult support. This kind of prolonged activation of the stress response systems can disrupt the development of brain architecture and other organ systems and increase the risk of stress related disease and cognitive impairment well into the adult years.

For most children who have experienced trauma and toxic stress, the experiences began at an early age. As a result, the events may be remote, and documented history is often buried among old records or nonexistent. Prenatal exposures that influenced brain development may not be detectable in obstetric records. Pediatricians should understand that presentations of attention deficits, emotional dys-regulation, and oppositional behaviors may have their roots in early abuse or neglect or other sources of toxic stress. Recognition of the power of early adversity to affect the child's perceptions of and responses to new stimuli may aid the pediatrician or other clinician in appropriately understanding the causes of a child's symptoms.

EFFECT OF TRAUMA ON PARENTING ABILITY
Adults who have experienced ACEs in their early years can

exhibit reduced parenting capacity or maladaptive responses to their children. The physiological changes that have occurred to the adult's stress response system as a result of earlier trauma can result in diminished capacity to respond to additional stressors in a healthy way. Adverse childhood experiences increase the chance of social risk factors, mental health issues, substance abuse, intimate partner violence, and adult adoption of risky adult behaviors. All of these can affect parenting in a negative way and perpetuate a continuing exposure to ACEs across generations.

An example of diminished parenting skills:
A mother, Anne*, has experienced multiple ACEs and was unable to deal effectively. She now has a child who is acting out in school or at home. Anne's inability to deal with her current high level of stress overloads her. As a result, she may punish/whip/cuss at her child in an extreme manner.

Another example would be:
A mother, Jessica*, is overwhelmed from her ACEs and she begins to gamble or drink excessively as a way to relieve her pain. As a result, she is unable to be present in the lives of her children.

Adverse experiences and other trauma in childhood, however, do not dictate the future of the child. Children survive and even thrive despite the trauma in their lives. For these children, adverse experiences must be counterbalanced with protective factors.

> *Adverse events and protective factors experienced together have the potential to foster resilience.*

These include healthy attachment relationships (especially with parents and caregivers), the motivation and ability to learn and engage with the environment, the ability to regulate emotions and behavior, as well as supportive environmental systems including:

- Education
- Cultural beliefs
- Faith-based communities

Examples would include making sure that a child exposed to trauma has the resources of: caring and loving caregivers and extended family members, church and spiritual communities, cultural identity, and becoming educated with solid information.

I took the ACE Study questionnaire and scored an eight out of ten. This means that I experienced all but two areas on the list. These included: An incarcerated family member and divorce. I chose to share my ACE story because I wanted to understand and heal myself, and to educate others on the effects of ACEs, and how IMPORTANT it is to deal with unresolved pain. I chose to break this generational curse because it is a part of my DESTINY to become transformed and stand as an example for others.

One important factor to consider now is that when you see a child or an adult "acting out," the question is not, "What's wrong with you?" but should be, "What happened to you?"
ENCOURAGEMENT

The impulse to keep one's truth, especially one's pain secretive is amongst the most powerful and toxic elements of human life.
The Pain to Power Principle states, *"Coming to grips with the*

truth rooted in our past is our greatest source of power." One of the ways we can learn to live the truth is by example. When we hear of someone who has shown the courage to look honestly at the most difficult chapters of her life story, you can be inspired to do the same.

Our journeys toward living the truth have the power to transform not just one life, but the lives of everyone around us. Your treasure is buried under chapters of your life story that you are too afraid to look at; chapters that taught you to settle for being less than you were created to be.

If you have unresolved trauma related issues, you MUST find the strength and courage to deal with them. Keeping the pain and suffering inside eats away at your soul and spirit and a part of your greatness dies.

I don't have to pretend that my life is or has been perfect. I believe that all the masking causes stress and depression. I don't mind that people know about my journey. As a matter of fact, I want to inspire and encourage healing. I don't have to prove anything or care what others say or think. I am finally comfortable with the newly transformed me. It matters only what I think about myself. After all this time, I now know that this is ALL that matters! And right about now, I absolutely love me and my life. It's peaceful, joyous, and perfectly imperfect! It's been a long road but I would not trade any part of the trip, because it's got me on my present path. The BIBLE says that God will exchange ashes for beauty and he is doing just that.

I made a conscious decision to share my ACE story, my lessons, testings, and blessings with the world. If I am able to help one person to become free of a painful past, then my moments of thinking that I would be opening my closet to the world is well worth the minor discomfort. It is my intention to educate women on the lifelong effects their decisions, actions, and behaviors will have over the lives of their children AND future generations. This is what the BIBLE calls family curses, and speaker and teacher, Iyanla Vanzant, calls pathology. Furthermore, it is also my intention that girls and women seek support by whatever means, so they will become authentic by facing the truth of who all aspects of themselves happen to be.

I now know that all of my experiences were a part of my soul's development in order to prepare me for my greatness. I didn't do anything wrong. My steps were ordered by the Creator and I grew through them so that the lessons would teach me to depend on myself. I trust and believe that the Universe has my back and is cheering for me every step of the way.

PRACTICES

I am taking a Spiritual/Mind Science method for healing. I have developed a morning ritual/practice of prayer and meditation. I read my Bible, make affirmations, burn incense, light candles, play music, and meditate. I have created a Sacred Space for Divine Love to shine its light on and through me. I welcome the space and presence for my healing to happen. Speaking, writing, and sharing my story with tips, tools, and techniques for healing, is soul fulfilling as well. I have learned who I am and know that I must use relaxation techniques and activities that I enjoy on a daily basis. You must make time for yourself daily and take care of yourself thus preventing feelings of overwhelm. I also love to research mind science which deals with how the conscious and subconscious mind operate. This helps me to reprogram my thinking for positivity and total well-being.

TIPS TO TRANSFORM YOUR LIFE

1. To Thine Own Self be True.
    Whenever we explain away our behaviors or sugarcoat the truth, we pay the consequences in the form of illness or drama. You cannot grow without it.
2. Welcome Change.
    Control often serves to reinforce our deep-rooted problems.
3. Come Clean.
    Stop living a Lie.
4. Forgive and Move On.
    Forgive yourself and then let it go.
5. Release Guilt and Shame.
    Address the Source of your guilt and shame. Remember that your experiences are a part of your Destiny!!
6. Celebrate your Successes!
    Acknowledge all of your victories at the end of each night. You are a courageous conqueror!!

TAKE CARE OF YOURSELF

- Seek help through a spiritual/religious path.
- Seek therapy or counseling.
- You may choose to do a combination of spirituality & therapy.
- Take time for yourself.
- Learn about Reiki and/or crystal energy healing.
- Talk to someone who is understanding.
- Learn about aromatherapy/essential oils.
- Get a spa massage OR whatever relaxes and makes you feel good AND is best for your HIGHER SELF.
- Get a Mani/Pedi.
- Look your best each day.

- Get your physical exams.
- Eat healthy meals.
- Listen to relaxing music.
- Take a walk.
- Work out.
- Ask for help.
- Watch a funny television program.
- Think about the things that you are grateful for.
- Journal.
- Find a support group.
- Become informed/Get educated.
- Learn about Grounding.
- Become a volunteer for an organization.
- Develop a Spiritual Practice or Ritual.
- Remain socially active, even if you don't feel like it.
- Join organizations or make new friends.

WHAT TO DO IF YOU ARE IN PAIN

For immediate crises and emergencies call 911.
Nami.org (800-950-6264 for support)
Healthywomen.org
Helpguide.org
Mentalhealthamerica.net
Bringchange2mind.org
Samhsa.gov
   (800-273-8255 Suicide Prevention)
   (800-6662-4357 Nat'l Help Line)

Most importantly: **Acknowledge your feelings and uncover why you feel that way. Develop a different perspective of looking at them. When possible, speak to someone who is understanding and refuse to allow issues to smother and** poison your soul. Do your work to bring a resolution to your painful past. Accept Divine Love as the most powerful healing force we can experience.

I plan to continue speaking, teaching, and writing books about Self-Development, Transformation, Spirituality, and "Living the Life You Crave." Look for my next project to be released soon!!

8

Confessions of an "Anti-Basic" Woman

Nakita "Nicci" Whittaker

Against the odds, Nakita "Nicci" Whittaker has consistently persevered in the face of adversity to become an inspiration to women regardless of age, ability and status. A teen mom who has suffered chronic illness, battled infertility, and now divorced after a 12 year marriage, Nicci has achieved what many would have deemed impossible by completing her higher education from Concordia University and is now an accomplished beauty expert and published author.

With over 15 years experience in marketing, event production, sales, branding and operations, Nicci has mastered a successful career as a media relations professional despite battling Lupus. Before being called to the beauty industry, she was featured in numerous publications such as RollingOut, The Forbes listed BOSS Network, Black Doctor.org and ChicagoNow.

LANIQUE Cosmetics is a unique merger of beauty and health. The LANIQUE line of mineral and hypoallergenic makeup offers a healthier option for women and is a ground breaking alternative to daily beauty routines. For years women who suffer from chronic illnesses like Nicci have had to compromise their beauty routines, dealing with the effects of harsh ingredients in high end cosmetics. LANIQUE provides an all-round solution that gives women the freedom to "enjoy being a girl."

LANIQUE is a brand designed to embrace all women regardless of chronic illnesses and obstacles which might leave them feeling any less beautiful than they really are. Ultimately, Nakita invites you to enjoy being you and "love oneself" unconditionally.

Website: www.laniquebeatybar.com
IG: @laniquebeautybar
FB: www.facebook.com/laniquebeautybar
Twitter: @NakitaWhittaker

"Every day, I wake up with the reality of knowing that I have a disease where there's no cure, and everyday can be my last. Yet, I manage to paint on a smile, throw on my finest stiletto's, dazzle my face in LANIQUE Cosmetics and Thrive Fearlessly throughout my day completely unbothered by my circumstances. It's been a long journey to get here, but I've managed the art of being "Anti - Basic."

Let Me Tell You What I Mean

I was diagnosed with Lupus in 2003. Lupus is an autoimmune disease that attacks various parts of the body at any time. What most people don't know about Lupus is that it comes in many forms and is extremely hard to diagnose. From memory loss and depression, to kidney failure - most people don't realize the pain and suffering of one who's diagnosed because most of us have grown accustomed to being "in pain" as our way of life. I am used to chronic hives, blood clots and blisters, hair loss, weight gain, and burning skin. I am used to being tired all of the time and forgetting my kid's names, etc... What I am <u>not</u> used to is failure or quitting, so I fight every day, not just for me but for other women who suffer from this disloyal disease as well.

What Does it Mean to Be "Anti-Basic"?

Being "Anti-Basic" is being confident, believing you are beautiful, that you are above your circumstances, you are fierce, and that you are anything but basic. Anti-Basic challenges your inner diva to go harder, go further, and maintain the attitude that failure is never an option.

Step Into My World

I am a career mom and divorced mother of 4 wonderful children. Clearly my path was not an easy one but it's my path and I have no regrets about it. My children are amazing, they keep me focused and grounded! Since being diagnosed with Lupus, I was also diagnosed with infertility. My doctors discovered that I had extremely elevated prolactin levels (imbalanced hormones), and coupled with stress makes it virtually impossible to conceive. After 7 years of unsuccessful attempts to bare children, my husband and I finally got pregnant with twins, Natalia and Terrance Jr. naturally and without any fertility treatments! These two are the epitome of a double bundle of joy. They came into my life in one of my darkest hours and saved me. Although our marriage ended, I am forever grateful to Mr. Whittaker for being my co-parent. My children give me life and they are the most prominent factors in my will to continue to exist. My second love is my career. I am the Founder and CEO of LANIQUE Beauty Bar and Cosmetics. LANIQUE Beauty Bar is a beauty blog and line of makeup and skincare that is dedicated to women with chronic illnesses. I share my journey, health and beauty tips, and most importantly, my own line of SPF 50, hypoallergenic Vitamin E based cosmetics.

I maintain life with this disease by telling myself every day, "Success is in my DNA, I will have a great day, I will not flare up," and I believe that.

> *The sooner we realize that we truly speak life, death, wealth, success and failure through our tongues, the sooner we will make better choices of our words.*

Life has not always been this easy. I had a very challenging road to get to where I am today. Allow me to take you on my journey.

From Teen Mom to Raising Teen Moguls
I had my first child at the young age of 18. Back then, I thought I

was in love and grown, but most importantly, I thought I was ready to start a family with the man who loves me. Today, I look back on this period of my life and say to myself, *"What in the hell was I thinking? A baby at 18 and with THIS ugly bastard??"* It's safe to say, that that fairytale idea was obviously short lived, so I immediately had to take an alternate route to finish my education, but I was determined to get it done and I did.

"My parents were very supportive, yet very clear that my son was <u>my</u> child and that I am responsible for his success and failures."

Knowing that and combined with my "baby daddy" leaving me to raise our son solo, I had to put on my big girl panties, wipe away those tears and keep thriving! I met a handsome young man named DaShon, who at the young age of 21, jumped in with both feet and became dad. Although our romantic relationship only lasted 5 years, DaShon is still a remarkable father to our now two amazing children: Jeriyon and DaShon Jr. Jeriyon is now 18 years old, a senior in high school, fashion guru and hard working man. DaShon is 16 and has his own video editing business (MVP Productions), with over 100,000 followers. And DaShon Sr. is a multi-award winning barber stylist and keeping our boys absolutely fly! Our primary focus in raising our children was ensuring they know to always DREAM BIG! Failure is never an option.

As a teen mom, I was fortunate enough to become a spokesmom for "Voices of Illinois Children," an advocacy group funded through the State of Illinois designed to provide resources for teen moms and motivate them to stay in school and not give up. This opportunity sprung many other entertainment gigs. I've been blessed with the opportunity to work on movie sets as well as film a few commercials. In 1998, my face was plastered on over 300 public transportation buses and trains, and viewed by millions of people every day. I guess you can say success really was in my DNA long before I realized it.

He Loves Me, He Loves Me Not - Pretty Much Sums Up My Love Life

It is said that we all encounter three great loves in our life. I truly believe I've met all three of them already, but I am not giving up hope for one day marching into the sunset and growing old with my King. These three men, who came into my life at different times, met a very broken, insecure yet very beautiful woman with the desire, interest and motivation to be a better person. However, I lacked resources and skill set to achieve that. I loved these three men with the very best in me, but sometimes your best just isn't good enough and that's okay. I guess it's safe to say with these three great loves, it walked hand in hand with my greatest heartbreaks I've ever experienced - which resulted in me building an emotional wall in my love life and a very strong issue with trust. The game of love is a process we all go through, as it tests our ability to love another person. Yes, I loved them all, but today I am currently in the best relationship. I am happy and complete and that relationship is with me. In order for you to love or accept love, you must learn to love and accept yourself first. I had to learn the hard way; you can't have a successful relationship with someone else until you've mastered the most valuable relationship within. Love yourself, love your flaws, accept your imperfections, and be with peace. I am currently in love with peace. I've actually loved peace since I was old enough to love. My advice to you all is to find your inner peace.

Managing Everyday Life with Pain

Lupus is a very unpredictable disease, I've had moments when I was completely fine, then hours later my skin is burning, body in arthritis type pain, hair loss, hives, etc. It took a while to figure out a daily routine for dealing with my body changes, but what I learned is that you have to pace yourself and know the signs of a flare-up long before it surfaces. Here's an example: I know a flare-up is underway when my migraines are more frequent than usual, or my inner thigh area tends to get inflamed. I had to learn to pace myself and be very careful to not overdo it. Know my limits, and never be afraid to say no. I had to realize that I can't attend every event, I can't always involve myself in my best friend's many heartbreaks, and getting involved in some careers are simply not conducive towards my health. The sooner I realized that, the easier life got for me. Stress is a killer in a class of its own; don't contribute to that by adding it to your persona because it's not worth it. Also be mindful that although you can't infect someone with Lupus, someone else's germs  can kill you. When friends and family are sick, I stay away if possible as my immune system isn't strong enough to fight off a virus as easily as a person without this illness. As a result, I have lost a few really good friends because they felt I wasn't there for them when they needed me, not understanding my disease is completely unpredictable. I have no regrets about that anymore, but it did contribute to a lot of sleepless nights and pain and suffering as a direct result of stressing about it. I have managed to keep a stable career and continued to build a firm foundation for my children by setting a strong example of no excuses.

Balancing Life, Career, and Lupus

I am determined to have as much of a normal life as possible. In achieving this, I must maintain the utmost diligence in maintaining a healthy routine and keeping my stress levels down as much as possible. I continue to take meds every day (all six pills), and I watch what I eat. From time to time I completely cut

red meat from my diet, as it's hard to digest. In addition, I keep soda to a minimum. For my hair loss, I use vitamin E powder capsules mixed with sulfur 8 pomade in my hair and I keep my skin hydrated in SPF-50 moisturizer or higher at all times. My support system consists of my family and friends who I love so much because they keep my grounded. I continue to update my blog regularly, as it is literally therapy for me to put my experiences on paper, and it allows me to continue to help others who suffer from this ill-mannered disease. I am now globally known for my transparent online journals that shed a new light on Lupus. I have been featured in magazines and online blogs country wide with a following now of 4 million viewers. I give all of the glory to God who is the head of my life. Without Him I am nothing. LANIQUE cosmetics is on path to making history with being one of only two cosmetic lines dedicated to women with chronic illnesses, and will also serve as a platform to raise awareness. I continue to look amazing daily because when you look good, you feel good. I am literally kicking Lupus's ass in my designer pumps. I will continue to thrive and smile fearlessly as I have accepted my victory at the start of my race for a cure. I told myself ahead of time, even the darkest hour is only 60 minutes so continue to live. So I whip my hair behind my ear, fling my designer handbag over my right shoulder, and I look at every challenge that comes my way in the eye and say,

"Try me...you won't win with the #Anti-Basic one!"

I want to thank my support system so much for keeping me grounded. I would like to first thank my parents, Jerry & Betty McGraw, for showing me how to survive. My beautiful and classy aunts, Juanita and Barbara, for being fabulous, beautiful and encouraging - my aunt and other mom Juanita (Dolly) told me when I was just a small child, that I would be Miss America one day. She told me I was beautiful at a young age and I believed her. My aunts and mom are true Proverbs 31 women and what I desire to be. I thank my amazing children for challenging me and keeping me youthful. I love you so much! The lovely Zondra Hughes of the Six Brown Chicks for helping me bring my story to life, and motivating me to have a voice. My W.T.F. sisters and Erika Gilchrist for the expert coaching and the sisterhood. The BOSS Network for being a team of amazing women who challenge me to be better. My boy's dad DaShon Sr. for having my back on so many occasions and telling me I'm great when I needed that voice. My Ex Husband Terrance for 12 years of co-parenting, and win or lose it's been one interesting ride. My support groups where I can go to vent about my health and receive good advice from people who actually understand what it is like to struggle with Lupus. My girlfriends - it is far too many of you ladies to name, but you know who you are and I thank you so much for being amazing and fabulous! My fellow butterflies, I fight for YOU! We will beat this together and our story is not done. My siblings, for being perfectly imperfect! My siblings are the only people who can see me at my worse and still manage to crack a joke, and I need that. Melly, believe it or not, I sincerely thank you for the experience and I am so happy to have met you. Our time together has taught me to step out on faith and LIVE. I love you for that. Knowing you has embarked a new chapter on my life - you were the absolute beginning to the new me. To my best friend Gerard, an 18 year friend and the one person who knew nothing of Lupus when I first told him about it. You're my friend who constantly researches cures, who serves as my meal coach, who challenges me to be a better person, and the undisputed Prince of Peace, LOL. I love you so much; you are certainly the light at the end of the tunnel...that smiling face and burst of positive energy, your selflessness knows no limits and for that, I am eternally grateful to have you in my life - even when we go years without talking. And lastly, to the person who is reading my story. I sincerely thank <u>you</u>. I hope you enjoyed my journey. Although, there is no cure for Lupus, it is not over. I am adding new chapters in my life daily and I am showing no signs of slowing down.

In life, we are all faced with challenges. It's how you handle them that determine the lesson. Stay focused, stay positive, and stay motivated. For you have the will, interest, and motivation to achieve any milestone you set. Trust the process; the challenge is the process. Don't worry about getting dirty during the process, focus on that beautiful diamond on the other side. Follow your #Anti-Basic Checklist and thrive!

My #Anti-Basic Checklist

- ✓ My Skin flares up - I create a cosmetic line #AntiBasic
- ✓ Lost my job in a male dominated industry - Became a CEO #AntiBasic
- ✓ Father of my child leaves - I make a way to care for him anyway #AntiBasic
- ✓ Had no car, begging for rides - I drive a Mercedes and Lexus #AntiBasic
- ✓ Hair falls out - I create a concoction to keep it in place #AntiBasic
- ✓ I've loved, I've lost, I've cried, I've smiled, I've won, I've

conquered, I've been lied to, I've been lied on, I've been cheated on, I've been sick, I've survived, but the one thing I can say that I haven't been is BROKEN! #AntiBasic

Life is precious, enjoy it! God never intended for any of us to live in bondage. I challenge the person who is reading this to rid yourself of that basic lifestyle. Have more confidence, be selfish sometimes, cut your hair, add some weave, paint your face, give a harmless wink to that hot guy at lemonade stand, take a trip alone, when someone tells you you're beautiful - believe them! But most importantly, step out of the ordinary and BE #AntiBasic!

9

Embracing the Pain of Transformation

Tiffany Winchester - Ford

Tiffany Winchester-Ford is a charismatic and multi-talented entrepreneur originally from the Windy City of Chicago, Illinois. As a humble, down-to-earth business woman, she continuously challenges herself and welcomes opportunities that compliment her brand. Ultimately, she wants her life to be her message which allows her to leave a legacy for her son.

After leaving her hometown, she moved to Alabama to attend college. It was there that she discovered her voice, her dreams, and her passion to build her brand, Winchester Ford Enterprises. As a Certified Coach, also known as "The Transformation-ista™," Tiffany now coaches other people on transformation. Drawing on over 16 years experience as a human resource professional, with certifications that range from Professional Trainer, Coach, to Professional Diversity Recruiter, her background in these areas provided the perfect foundation for her business. Tiffany now focuses mainly in the following subject areas: life, career and relationships. She continuously challenges herself and has added published author, actress, model, and fashion designer to her growing resume.

Tiffany is also a big advocate and supporter of adoption. As an infant, she was adopted and raised by two loving parents.

Tiffany is a devoted wife and dedicated mother. She currently lives in Atlanta, Georgia with her husband, Randall. They have a son name Jamison "Jamie" Ford. Some of her favorite quotes are "Leave people better than you found them," "You create your own opportunities," "Build your character and master your skills," and "Be the change."

www.winchester-ford.com
@transformationista

> *It's been said that the best thing you can give a child is a loving home, with loving parents. But what if I told you that that simply isn't enough? Allow me to explain...*

I am moved to tears as I write this because I realize just how long I've held on to my emotions. I tried so hard not to feel, until I was numb. The void I've come to terms with has finally caught up with me and every time I look in the mirror, I am reminded that it still exists. For many years, I tried to hold it all together, but my soul would not allow me to live in denial any longer. I was forced to stand front and center with who I was. I reluctantly acquiesced with the affects that it had over my life for many years. Lord, I just ask that you to give me the strength to continue to write this.

I wonder if anyone ever noticed how much we resembled. She stood about 6-foot-tall and he was just shy of 6 feet. They would soon discover how much they shaped my life forever. It never dawned on me then, that one day I would eventually feel the need to share my story. I often wondered what my life would've looked like had I not been adopted.

You Loved Me, but You Left Me

I hurt because you gave up on me. You have never seen my smile. You have never felt my hugs. You have never heard my voice. You were never there to celebrate my wins in life or hold me at my lowest. I was forced to write "unknown" on forms that asked about my medical history or what may run in my family's history. You could never know how that feels. Being separated at any age from your mother is devastating. To be separated at birth by your mother leaves a lasting impact on a baby because a baby needs the comfort of what is familiar and to share in the bond with its mother. The relationship with whom I was most intimate was forever severed. Where is my mom? Where's my dad? What is my identity? Where do I belong? Do I have siblings? Who am I? I think a part of me will always be waiting for you. Why did you leave? I have struggled with these questions for many years. I acted as if I really didn't care and was unaffected by it when asked.

You left your baby girl in a hospital full of strangers after giving birth and that was the last time we saw one another. Despite the fact that you gave me up, I was taught, in my faith, to love you anyway. You gave someone else a chance to be a mother and a father. I completely understand the logical reasoning of such a selfless act, which turned out to be a blessing. It does not, however, remove the emotional void that has plagued my life for so many years. I ultimately realized that I was unwilling to channel any deeply rooted emotions because I didn't want to feel unwanted, rejected or abandoned. But I will no longer deny these feelings because they are valid and they do exist. I didn't just lose one parent, I lost them both. How do **two people** decide they don't want the child that they created together? What the hell?

Throughout my life, it became increasingly difficult for me to escape. For so long, I had so many unanswered questions. I had no sense of self. People say that when a parent gives their child up for adoption that it is out of love. You loved me but you left me, never to return. This is not to say that I am not eternally grateful for the souls that God chose to walk in, choose me, and to raise me as their very own. I owe them my life. They are my parents in every sense of the word and I have always adored them. They have forever shaped my life and I was blessed to have an amazing childhood.

Revelation

Over the years, it might've appeared to some, that I had it all together, but that was not the case. I never opted to discuss my adoption because I don't believe I ever truly accepted it. It wasn't that I was ashamed of it; I just didn't feel connected to it. I swept it under the rug because I didn't know how to describe what I felt. I had mixed emotions. I thought that if I didn't speak about it, then it didn't exist. Nonchalance and avoidance became my default and that is how I coped with most things that I wasn't prepared to "deal" with, unfortunately.

I eventually went on to college and it was there that I discovered an indescribable void. I recall a specific time while sitting around with friends watching daytime television. I remember watching an episode that was airing at the time, which dealt primarily with a reunion of a family. The family hadn't seen their child since she was put up for adoption. It gave me chills and I was trying my best to hold back the tears. It was a surreal moment for me. It was so quiet in the room you could hear a pin drop. Everyone was so engaged in the show. Later, a friend asked if I had ever thought about searching for my biological family. At that time, I could honestly say that it had never crossed my mind. I'm not sure if it was the show or the thought of someone actually asking me about it that stuck with me, but it's been on my mind every day since. It was a pivotal point in my life. I will never forget that day. Unbeknownst to me, it was the day that I gave birth to something that had been festering inside of me for some time.

The Great Void

There was an indescribable void, an emptiness, if you will. I am told that many adoptees share a similar void. It is indescribable. I look back over my life at so many decisions I've made. Many of them somehow link directly and others indirectly to this void. I was trying to fill this empty space in my life with material possessions and with people who could never fill it. What an unfair weight to place on their shoulders! My life was one big, tumultuous world wind that had turned into a vicious cycle. I lost control many years ago. This overwhelming lack of "belonging" had manifested in ways that were very self-destructive:

➤ Searching for love in all the wrong places
➤ Destroyed credit (debt)
➤ Depleted finances (broke)
➤ Over-eating, obesity (self-sabotage)
➤ Lack of independence (dependency)
➤ Failure (all areas of my life)

I felt abandoned by my biological parents. Rejection, coupled with uncertainty, caused a myriad of feelings and emotions. Because of this, I wasn't quick to let people go. No matter how they treated me, I didn't want to abandon them. I held on for dear life. You could say that I loved hard. I would always look for that one reason to stay, the good in them. I looked for their potential. I loved others more than I loved myself. I was a champion for others. I was seeking acceptance from people because I longed for a sense of belonging. What a sad existence.

Long-term relationships with men I had dated were never enough to remove what was missing in my life. I hadn't dealt with it up close and personal before. The relationships held no substance in my life and lacked everything I needed to feel appreciated and genuinely loved in return. Being mistreated in relationships was just another issue I had to deal with and I could see an ugly cycle occurring. I knew I couldn't continue on this way. It took one last straw to eventually break the camel's back, and it was well over 10 years in the making. I had finally had enough. I had wasted so many years on guys who could never give me the love that I deserved. Hell, I didn't even love myself enough to know the difference. I look back on the dumb shit I did, the shame and embarrassment and just shake my head. I was done being mistreated, lied to, unappreciated and disrespected. It was time. If I ever wanted anything good in my life, then I had to hold myself accountable and run like hell. There was no turning back. I felt like Tina Turner when she ran for her life after the car incident with Ike. It felt liberating and in that moment I felt free. A huge burden was lifted and it felt good. I took back my life and I got back up.

Perfectly Imperfect

A few years later and soon after a plethora of bad decisions and unhealthy relationships, I found myself repeatedly hitting a dead end. I was working a part time job, living pay check to pay check and couldn't afford to live anywhere. I had destroyed what little credit I had and didn't have anything saved. I slept on a few friend's couches, and air mattresses. I eventually ended up living in a hotel for the next 2 years of my life. I had exhausted every possible resource I had. At that point, all I could do was be still. With no real sense of direction, I was feeling insecure, unfocused, alone and incomplete. My spirit was completely broken and my soul was close to empty, but my heart was still beating. I didn't realize how bad off I was until I had lost my independence. I knew something had to change.

I was living a reckless life and was trying to overcompensate for the void that had subconsciously become all too familiar. I was lost, and unhappy. I didn't completely understand what I was feeling. Eventually, I began to grow numb to many of my emotions. I chalked it up as a common life experience, the hand that I was dealt.

> *I have always known that I was a good person. I just didn't know how to be good to myself.*

I didn't love myself enough to even know what I deserved. The men I chose looked nothing like my dad. He was very respectable, a provider, and a gentleman with southern charm and humor. I sacrificed respect in order to be accepted and liked. I was missing something so significant in my life and I had no idea where to find it.

My life was passing by so quickly and I had nothing to show for it. Meanwhile, I was growing older and had seen my life pass by a few times. I felt alone, ashamed and I began to grow distant and weary. I just needed a handle on life.

Through it all, I just wanted to know why my biological family never came for me. Dammit, where were they?!?!? I just wanted to know how their lives turned out, what they looked like, their likes and dislikes, and who they were – which would ultimately help me to understand who I was. I wondered for many years where they were. Why didn't they come looking for me? Do they think about me? Do they even care? I attempted to start the journey to search for them on numerous occasions, but every time I'd finish filling out the paperwork, I would convince myself not to go through with it. I would always find a reason not to do it. What if they didn't want to find me? What if they hadn't even informed their current family about me? I would hate to be rejected again. What if they are deceased? I didn't know if I could deal with that. I just couldn't fathom dealing with all the "what ifs." I just figured I'd leave it alone.

Farewell Caterpillar. Hello Wings!

After a multiplicity of hardships and disappointments, I yearned for independence, self-improvement and success. I made a decision that has affected the course of the rest of my life. I decided that I did not want to be a victim. I refused to be defeated. I did not want to be where I was in my life any longer. I made the choice to pour every bit of energy into my life and my dreams.

Married Mom on the Move

Fast forward 10 years, I eventually married my best friend and gave birth to our son shortly after. At a time when I was feeling pretty good about myself and the progress that I was making, a once genuine friendship began to blossom. It was the most precious friendship because it was so innocent, unfamiliar, yet, very refreshing. I respected this man and loved spending time with him. It just felt right and certainly nothing that I've ever felt before. I knew he had a lot of love for me because he showed me. The feelings were mutual. He wasn't like any of the others I had previously allowed into my world. He was far from perfect but he was perfect for me.

I was so busy trying to repair myself and pick up the pieces in my life that I was resistant at first. Neither of us wanted to tarnish our friendship. It was just too valuable and we had that much respect for it.

Despite the 9-year age difference, we deeply cared and valued one another. We didn't want to rush into things; we just enjoyed the journey together. My career was growing and my life was becoming more stable. I was finally experiencing a new chapter in my life. How refreshing! I just wanted to remain focused on my personal goals and maintain perspective of everything.

My son, who is the only blood relative that I know, is my greatest joy. I was growing and reconnecting to my faith by attending a local church that I soon grew to love. I decided to give it a chance because I was blown away by the Pastor and his message. Growing more spiritually, as a wife and as a mother, I began to examine other areas of my life as well. When you have a little person counting on you, you make it happen, by any means necessary. I began to see my life transforming. You see, God had already shown me that He was there and had always been there. I just hadn't connected to Him. I had not prayed to Him and I had very little faith in Him.

When I changed my view on life, prayed about it, and started doing the work to fix myself, I was eventually able to focus on the life that I wanted. I was moved by my spirit to make some changes:

- I began sowing seeds of greatness, not just around me, but in others as well.
- I started envisioning my life the way I wanted it to be, not the way that it once was.
- I slowly began to believe in myself and changed the way I spoke over myself. (I can vs. I can't)
- I began changing the words that I used to describe who I was.
- I started doing the work and putting my life together.
- I began taking on some of the challenges I thought I felt would always hold me back.

- I had to isolate myself to evolve and grow.
- I looked forward and kept going even if I got knocked down.
- I refused to quit!

The Evolution of Tiffany

I looked to God for guidance and for the platform to stand on in the midst of the storm. I'm going through a storm as I write this, but I am using this platform to show you that there will be storms in your life. I don't care how much you've "fixed" yourself or you've prayed. The storms will come. It's what you do in the midst of the storm that helps gets you through it. I held my head up high and stretched my arms to Him. You see, when you make the decision to change the direction of your life, you will no longer be held to the level you once were. You begin to grow and shift your mental state. Your overall well-being becomes a top priority. Your quality of life alters it is then that you begin to pick up the pieces. Get rid of the notion that you have no options, no voice, and no more fight. You become your own best friend and you begin to evolve. A transformation occurs.

I began to speak less about the issues and more about the lessons and the blessings in them. See, I could never change the issues or my past, but, I could change the outcome. I slowly began to heal. When you see *yourself* differently, others begin to see you differently as well. The desires of your heart will eventually be redirected, and your soul reignited. You will be on fire for the ultimate fight for your life. I get excited just thinking about it because it all came down to a simple decision.

I literally began to hold myself accountable by busting my ass to hustle for the life I wanted. Enough with the reasons why I couldn't do something, beating myself up, or using fear to determine my worth. I decided to be amongst the living. I made the choice to take my life back. I welcomed challenges and learned to work through them. The mind is a very powerful thing. Quit talking yourself out of doing things. Quit living in fear and telling yourself what you can't do.

I have always shown up for everyone else. I decided to finally show up for myself. My happiness and purpose-filled life was on the line. There was no more getting comfortable at that point. I couldn't allow fear, past hurt or denial to run my life. I refused to allow it to dictate who I would become. My biggest challenge has always been myself.

Life is about choices. Listen, it wasn't that I was escaping my feelings, I just made a choice not to beat myself up any longer. There are things that we have absolutely no control over and there are things that we can control. One thing that I could control was my own stinking thinking. I just had to put on my big girl panties and fight like hell for my life. I had to do some soul searching and tap into a myriad of deeply rooted emotions that had been suppressed for some time. I literally had to isolate myself from everyone and everything that I "thought" I needed in my life in order to do so.

I look back over my life and realize how far I've come. I did the work and was ready for the world. I began to channel my energy towards God. I know it

> *I now know all about the struggle, which was designed solely to build you, not __break__ you.*

was God who pulled me through. I won't lie and say that I don't have questions from time to time, or that I don't yearn for the unknown, with regard to my biological family. I acknowledge how far I've come and through it all; I have discovered myself. I trust God and I am grateful for everything that He has done in my life.

Today, I am focused on making myself a priority, being the best wife and mom that I can be, and I can't thank God enough. I have gone on to run an awesome businesses and I won't stop until I am soaring with the eagles. If you had asked me who I was a few short years ago, I'd say, "A total mess." Today, I would tell you that I know exactly who I am:

I am a Child of God
I am Adopted
I am a Woman
I am a Daughter
I am a Wife
I am a Mother
I am a Friend
I am an Entrepreneur
I am a Survivor
I am a Married mom on the move
I am a Transformationista™
I am Unbreakable

The Power of Transformation

Today, I am so grateful. I love who I am becoming. I decided to take on the many challenges that I once felt would hold me back. I have created my own opportunities, gained my independence back, and have learned that happiness is an inside job.

I soon learned over time to trust the process and to push through. There is a lesson or a blessing in everything. There is unspeakable joy just to know this. I have learned that the journey is just as important and as rewarding as the destination. Our life is our testimony and should be our message to the world. Embrace it.

One might inquire about "the unsent letter". Well, I look forward to the day that I drop it in the mail and begin the search for my biological family. I no longer worry about the "what ifs." I know that whatever the experience or outcome, it is a valuable part of my journey. Due to my newfound wisdom and strength, I know that I can handle it. My story is just beginning and I am thrilled about the possibilities. To be continued...

This was written from my heart - the good, the bad and the ugly. I wrote transparently about a very long and personal period of struggle, denial, self-love and fear in my life. In doing so, it will inadvertently open doors to the opinions and judgments of others. I am in a place now where I'm okay with that. These days, it is difficult to shake me because I am hard to rattle. I wrote about these significant stories in my life because I know I can't be the only one. I can only hope that it is received and felt. As therapeutic as this writing experience has been for me, it took a lot of energy. I hope that it will enrich someone's life and I pray that it has great impact. My greatest reward would be that it inspires someone to connect to their faith, do the work, make better choices, evolve on their own terms, love themselves first, thrive fearlessly and to push through.

This is my life at age 43, "Transformed."
Perspective. Clarity. Wisdom. Understanding.

10

Fearlessly "Bitter Sweet"

Treanice Johnson
A.K.A. "Trea Bertrille"

A victim of domestic violence, traumatized as a child, abandoned by her father and unfaithful husband, Treanice was able to cultivate faith in her life that allowed her to develop a strong connection with her Heavenly father. Treanice managed to thrive, accomplish her goals, and beat the odds that was projected by her family and peers. She lives outside the box and she's forever an unstoppable woman! Treanice Johnson, earned her Master's degree in Computer Science in 2008. She's a professional IT Specialist, Business Owner, Actress, Lifestyle Model, and Author. Her family roots in New Orleans, Louisiana, born in N. E. Washington, DC and raised in different parts of Maryland. This chapter sums up different events in her life and covers how she got through the challenges that faced her while accomplishing her goals. This is only the beginning of books to come. She has committed herself to strive for innovative ways to share experiences and to help others to "Thrive Fearlessly!" I dedicate this book to people who have and are going through life pains and struggles; you're not in this alone, don't give up the race, there's light at the end of the tunnel. Well, here's my story!

Treanice Johnson
AKA, Trea Bertrille
Co-Author

When Life Gives You Lemons
Add Some Sugar & Keep Pushing!

"When life gives you lemons make lemonade," says the old optimistic proverbial phrase, first coined by Elbert Hubbard in 1915. Life will bring many challenges whether it's with self, relationships, family, work, your spiritual faith, health, testing your mental strength, or finding time to manage it all. Just know there's light at the end of the tunnel.

Dealing with Self Issues

Before I let you know who I am, let me start by saying, "It doesn't matter where you start; it's how you end!!" If I can make it and be successful, you can too! I was very quiet, shy and timid growing up, and I was also the middle the child. I had shutdown due to domestic violence that was going on during my adolescence years. I stayed to myself, and I had no interest in anything. Emotionally, I just wasn't there – I was angry and sad and didn't care about anything. It was like I was an empty shell.

Do you know what it feels like to be living like an empty shell? If not, I can tell you that it's like being <u>lifeless</u> inside! I really fell behind in school; nobody cared and I didn't either. When I saw my mom and dad fight that was the end of me – I felt heartbroken. My dad left and didn't look back. I would cry myself to sleep. When I was 8 years old, I threatened to run away from home and my mom would tell me, "Go ahead!" I had this big old box ready to go too. She knew that I wasn't going anywhere with that big box, but to an 8 year old, I felt like she didn't care so I was going. They didn't know I was contemplating ending my life. I was thinking of every way to carry it out that wasn't so painful. This thinking went on at many stages of my life, feeling abandoned and no one cared.

When I was 12 years old, my mom got re-married and it was starting all over again. This was going on all of my adolescent years. Domestic violence really took a toll on me and severely affected my life; I hate violence of any sort. As a victim, it took years to heal mentally, emotionally, and to understand and stop blaming myself. It was like a whole big chunk of my life was stolen from me. At age 15, I hung around the wrong crowd and made some very bad decisions - I experimented with different things that the average teen experiments with: smoking weed on my birthday, skipping school, being defiant...etc. The school I attended was a lot like putting ghetto kids in the suburbs with the stuck-up kids. Of course there were fights popping off all the time. It was such a challenge for me to learn in that type of environment. One time I saw a kid sitting on the bleachers who was very stylish. Sort of like the GQ type. This guy from the other side of town came from out of nowhere and punched the boy in the face. Honestly, I can't see how anybody got a valuable education in that school. I had my share of fights and I was tested more than I ever wanted to be. I didn't fight every fight, some didn't belong to me. They belonged to God - at least that's what I was taught. I read 2 Chronicles 20:15 and that's what kept me peaceful and grounded. Reading the bible kept me from being ignorant, ghetto, and a wild savage bunny.

I was 18 and slowly awakening and now growing into myself, "God really does give beauty instead of ashes," Isaiah 61:3. I would look around and I saw people my age going off to college and growing in their lives, and it was time for me to grow out of this box I felt like I was in. I started having bible studies and reading different books that would promote positivity. I enrolled in Community College and passed my Civil Service test and got into the Federal Government learning the work force. I would pray and ask God to draw close to me, heal me, and I begged Him to forgive me and help me to forgive those who trespassed against me. I also asked Him to make me into the woman He would want me to be and also how to be a blessing to others.

My friends were older and more experienced than me and when I look back, I don't know why in the heck I hung around those women. They were into drugs, drinking, shop lifting, whatever – pretty much living the street life. At that time it seemed pretty cool to me. They were pretty women who like to look good and had a lot of men wanting them. Back in high school they used to always pick with me about being a virgin. That's why I had my first child at 18 and then another 3 years later. That lifestyle caused me to lose my good government job. If only I had known then what I know now! On one occasion, I caught contact from those "white boys," known as laced marijuana. My heart was racing and it wouldn't slow down. I'd heard about people running down the street butt naked and hiding underneath the bed, and I was determined that was not going to me, not that night. I screamed out and asked God to help me!

I saw one of my home girls flip out in the car from smoking that stuff, and the police pulled us over. All I could remember was that she was scratching the ground, jumping up and down talking about she had to pee. The police was searching the car for drugs, and helicopters were flying over our heads right in the middle of downtown DC. It was funny as heck at the time. I know we were on TV that night, but that was enough! I learned that you have to really be careful of who's influencing your life. I could have been retiring at an early age if I kept my government job. But now I had to quickly get myself together because I had two kids and no job. I enrolled in a business college at the age of 24, where I met my ex-husband. Here I am playing catch up, applying myself, and learning that all I can. I even surprised myself when I got my test results from school. The good marks pushed me to work even harder. I started having my bible studies with Jehovah's Witnesses, and I decided to get baptized. That was a very precious time in my life. To me, that confirmed my progress and the close relationship between me and my heavenly Father.

Remember, my physical father had abandoned me, and my heavenly Father took his place. Why does it seem like when things are going well the worst things seem to happen? I found out that my ex-husband had got some woman pregnant...damn! I wanted to kill him. The pain I felt was indescribable, not to mention the shame and embarrassment. At the time I had known him for 13 years, and we were married for 4 of those 13 years. He wanted us to stay together and take care of his baby - I don't think so!!

I know that we had our disagreements, but how could he have done this to me?! I was a good wife and a good mother - just unbelievable. But he had been verbally and physically abusive to me. If we weren't arguing and fighting about finances, it was about women, sex, religion or the kids. This was my ticket out of this craziness! When he told me that he had gotten some woman pregnant that was it! We separated, and that's when my depression started. I would push myself to work, making meetings and field service as a requirement of being a JW. But slowly, I stopped attending my meetings and became in active. It was very hard on me, and Satan was attacking me in areas of my life home, work and my family. I really couldn't find a place where I fit in anywhere and be at peace. It was beginning to be a bit too much for me to handle. But I kept pushing, going to work, and doing what I needed to do to get by and then it happened. I met this guy who came in to work on my computer, and my life shifted!

Relationships

He was a sight for sore eyes - fine and educated. We would talk and laugh at work and then he asked me for my number, so I gave it to him. My ex-husband cheated on me and had gone about his business, so why not?! He would call me and we would talk for hours. We would meet up and have sex every chance we could. It was hot and steamy! The things we would do...I was pretty much over my ex-husband. I fell in love with this man. I guess I was trying to find a way to escape from reality by putting my feelings into someone else. Besides, my marriage was dysfunctional and it felt good at the time. We were 3 months well into the relationship and my dream man called me to tell me that he had something to tell me. I met up with him with butterflies in my stomach. I was thinking, "I hope this isn't bad news, it feels too good to end now." He began talking, "T., I'm married! I've been separated for some time now and I still live with her, but in the basement. I'm there just until I get my money together to leave and move into my own house. I'm in love with you, and I hope you stay around. I really enjoy your company." All I heard at that time was, "I'm married." I couldn't believe what I was hearing! My heart fell to the floor, and even worse is that I don't even remember asking him if he was married. I didn't see a ring.

I'm having mixed feelings now, even though my ex-husband and I were separated. I felt just as low as he should have been feeling. I should have cut it off, but my rationale was that we were both in bad marriages, found each other and was going to make it work. Nobody's perfect and there's always something you will have to deal with. So I guess it's a matter of what you're willing to put up with. This guy would pay my rent, buy food for the kids, and co-signed for a car, so I could turn in the van that my ex-husband had co-signed for. He was actually trying to make plans with me. He was taking me around his family; we were always going out, and spending lots of time together. I can recall our Ocean City trip when he took his kids from his first marriage, along with mine, for a weekend of fun. Incidentally, that's also where I found out about his new baby by his first wife. Here we go again...

A Good Thing Ended

I kind of sensed that his children wanted their parents back together – which is understandable. We were all sitting down while their dad went to the bathroom, so I asked them how they were doing in school. They were between 8 and 13 years old, bright, and well-mannered kids. They were always laughing like something was up. I couldn't see it then, but I can see it now. So, they responded that they were "good" and they spoke about their grades, their mom, and their little baby brother. I asked what his name was and they told me with a smile on their face and they all had same last name. I looked away in disbelief.

Putting two and two together, he must have been cheating on his present wife with his first wife. I be got damn!! Oh, so **_that's_** why he would write all those child support checks! I didn't want to spoil the trip, so I waited to talk to him about it when we got home. The weekend came to an end and we dropped the kids off. Later on that evening, I told him about the conversation that I had with his kids which revealed that his baby had the same last name as the others. "They told me, now I'm asking you. Why does your first wife youngest son have your last name?" He told me that after their divorce she kept his last name, so when the baby was born he took his last name and he told her that she needed to get that fixed. What woman would believe that sh*t?!! We broke up and clearly he must have been seeing someone else while seeing me. It didn't take long for him to find and marry someone else and move her and her kids into the house that we were looking to buy together. I truly believed that I dodged a bullet. God works things out for our good!

As time went on, I just found out so much stuff about this dude from his many women. Eventually, I had to let that go and pursue other things. The relationship was becoming more than I could handle, and the pain I felt at times was overbearing and took a lot of strength to get through it. The lesson I learned was: *Give yourself time to heal before moving on to something else.* It can become a vicious cycle and accumulate additional baggage that you have to sort through that can take years to repair. The Huffington Post states, "Jumping into another relationship right away is like covering the pimple with concealer instead of applying medication and allowing it enough time to heal." After we broke up, I started facing different challenges with my family.

Family

I have three children - one son and two daughters, all 3-4 years apart. After my divorce, I struggled as a single mother working a full time job, keeping the bills paid, and food on the table. I also attended a University full time. All of my family has put me through some type of heartbreak and it seemed like they were working against me. But I met some new friends while trying to rebuild my life.

Things were going well until I received a call that my son was caught with firearms that belong to the police, oh boy! That wasn't the only thing that was going on. My daughter was raped by a guy she had a crush on, and the other one was sneaking off from school. Meanwhile, I was being sexually harassed passively by my professor, and also harassed by this lady at work. I thought, "Oh My God! How much can a person take?!" I fell down to my knees and prayed to my God with tears in my eyes asking for strength, relief, direction and to hold me back from hurting someone.

Right away, a peace came over me and I had to make some quick decisions. Find a good lawyer for my son, get my daughter into counseling, and send my other daughter to her father's house for a little while. I had to switch classes, and report this lady to the division chief. A self-growth article stated, "It's not what happens to us, but our response to what happens to us that makes the difference." I wanted to be successful, so I kept pushing. Situation + Response = Outcome. Soon after, I was promoted at work, and received a Master's of Science in Enterprise Resource Management. My son now owns a Landscaping business, my daughter is a License Cosmetologist, and the other daughter is a Certified Nursing Assistant. Praise God!

Work
I plan on retiring early to be with my family. Yes, I'm very ambitious. I hang around with millionaires because I plan to be a millionaire through my acting, modeling and as a business

owner. I have all these projects I'm working on that will get me there sooner rather than later.

Remember, I'm playing catch-up. If you want to be successful, it requires successful thinking. I get very excited about what I'm doing and I know that I am "success" in the making. The current issues that I'm experiencing are with drama prone people. Co-workers won't mine their business and trying to put up road blocks, jealous family members spreading vicious rumors that turn other family members against me and causing division, and I tell them, "Ain't nobody had it easy!!" You have to go and get yours, while blessing people on the way! Luke 6:28 "Bless those who curse you, pray for those who mistreat you." Genesis 12:2 "I will make you into a great nation. I will bless you, and you will be a blessing to others." The Four Laws of God's Blessing States, "Our blessings should flow to others."

Faith

Making time for God, putting God first and making time to fulfill commitments and obligations is the path to peace. Oh my heavenly Father, how can I ask you to bless and protect me, if I don't give you my time? I started going back to worship service, trying a different denomination now, and encouraging my kids and people who haven't come to know God to do so. Matthew 6:33 states, "Seek first His kingdom and His righteousness, and He will give you everything you need." When you develop your faith and have great faith in God, your life will begin to get better, you will make wiser decisions, you will start to look younger, you will see life differently, and chains will break loose. Cultivate love for yourself and people; what you put out into the Universe comings back 10 fold. Make it a habit to bless someone each day and God's face will shine upon you and doors will open for you from God's favor. What God gives you, no one can take it away!! Don't look and be jealous of what someone else has. Instead, believe that He has something amazing for you and visualize that you have received it and you will receive it!! He will come when you call Him and provide escape for you! Everything good that comes from God, no one can take it away!! Just remember that! Cultivate the fruits of the spirit and write it on your heart!

Health

 The Daily Health Wire article, *Three Reasons to Maintain Good Health*, states that if your health isn't good, nothing's good. Eating right, hitting the gym at least three times a week, and getting proper rest and regular check-ups will help in preventing bad health. Allowing stress and a bad diet in your life with no exercise can cause:

- Anxiety
- Diabetes
- high blood pressure
- Obesity

I'm a woman who "Thrives Fearlessly" and I want to be successful in every area in my life.

Mental Strength

If your mind isn't right, it could interfere with your performance in being successful. With all the lemons that life has thrown at me, I would need to see a psychiatrist. However, I would read online articles from *Life Script.com*, where *I read some* good mental health tips. I began to hang with good positive people and when I lost my dad, positive and understanding people helped me to get through it. Also, choosing what I allowed in my mind and cultivating a mental strength that no one can penetrate, positions me to thrive beyond my wildest dreams. Anyone can be violent, but the one who can control a situation where both people can win are champions. Remember, Satan will attack your talents so protect them. For me, it's love for people – you know they can do things to make you hate them! The things and situations I've gone through with people, I've could have been a killer with no remorse. Satan worked on me from a little child starting with my parents being selfish not seeing about me. I didn't allow him to change the loving person I am today. Educate yourself, find your niche, and boldly display your talent! John 10:10 states, "We have a greater enemy, who we can't see, but he works through ignorant people to carry out his will and that is to kill and destroy as many people as he can." Revelation 12:12 says, "He only has a short time left, before he's destroyed, he hates you."

Closing

I would like to inspire people from all walks of life to make positive changes in their lives and go out and get what they want. In order to achieve my goals, I had to develop and heal the child within, forgive people, end a bad relationship, support and give direction to my kids, and be a blessing to others. Now I see a breakthrough by putting first God in every area of my life. Finally I'm winning! Thank you Almighty God, my life is dedicated to you and you're my light at the end of the tunnel!!

11

The Day My Angel Received Her Wings

Vicki Lynn Olds

 Vicki Olds was born on August 7, 1966 in Chicago Illinois. She was raised by two loving middle class parents who stressed getting a good education. She attended St. Margaret of Scotland Elementary School, Academy of Our Lady High School & Columbia College where she received her degree in Journalism. After college she decided not to pursue a career in journalism right away. She started a career in Corporate America instead where she spent the next 25 years.

Over those 25 years Vicki married and had a beautiful daughter Nikki who was the love of her life. She did everything with Nikki, took her to all of her dance recitals, chess matches, girls scout outings, school plays, school concerts etc. Vicki is the President of the Smile for Nikki Foundation, which was founded on July 9, 2015 following Nikki's death.

Vicki is eternally grateful for the support that she has received for her foundation which was setup in her daughter Nikki's honor. Vicki has established a new found strength after losing her only child in a tragic accident. Through this horrible experience, Vicki has navigated her daily life by being a woman who thrives fearlessly.

Email: v.olds@smilefornikki.org
Website: www.SmileForNikki.org
Office: 219-789-1988

Friday May 29, 2015 started out just like any other spring morning that year. The sun was shining, the sky was blue, and it was a balmy 75 degrees. My daughter Nikki and I got up to prepare for our weekend. She read her bible, did her yoga, fed Max (our toy Terrier), showered, and prepared our juice for the morning. I packed my clothes for my weekend stay at my fiancé (Johnny's) home, showered and got dressed. Once I was dressed I went and sat in the kitchen with Nikki so we could talk about our weekend plans. She informed me that she was going to be around the house most of that weekend after Friday because this was her boyfriend Russell's weekend away for National Guard. So after babysitting during the day she would be home. Me being the Mom I am I told her "Okay." Well, you know the drill; keep me posted via text message or call if anything changes. She replied as usual, "I know I know I know Mother I will."

I told her that my fiancé and I were going to a concert that evening to see Michelle Ferrell. She stated that it sounded like fun!!!! "You can tell me all about it tomorrow when we talk." Afterwards, we finished discussing our plans for the weekend.

Nikki said, "Ma, go ahead and pack up the car while I put Max up and lock up." I looked at her for a second because usually she always pulled the car out of the garage and I locked up. But I didn't say anything. I went and pulled the car out. Nikki got in the car and we drove off listing to music on her phone. We sang, talked, and laughed all the way to Johnny's house.

40 minutes later we pulled into Johnny's driveway, and unloaded the car. Nikki came in for just a minute because she was running a little behind schedule for her babysitting job. She grabbed a bottle of water from the refrigerator, gave me my huge hug and a big kiss. I walked her out to the car and gave her my speech,

"Text me as soon as you get there and don't forget." She replied in her funny yet nonchalant way, "I know I know I know Mom." I told her, "I love you Sweetpea," as I always did whenever I would leave her or end a phone conversation with her. She replied, "I love you too Mom." As Nikki drove away with her huge smile on her face, I watched her from the end of the driveway as I often would do until I couldn't see her anymore.

After she left I came into the house and started unpacking as I did every weekend. I called Johnny to let him know that I was at his house and we talked briefly. I asked him what he wore to work so I would know what to wear to the concert that night. After I finished my conversation with Johnny, I realized that I hadn't heard from Nikki yet so I gave her a call. When she answered I asked her if she was ok and if she had arrived yet. She stated that she was just pulling into the driveway because there was a lot of traffic on the expressway. I said ok with a sigh of relief because I know that she was only 20 minutes from Johnny's house and 45 minutes had gone by. I told her to have a great day and to text me when she got home. "And Mommy loves you Sweetpea!" She replied, "I love you too Mom."

That was around 10:00 am Friday morning. I went about the rest of my day at Johnny's house, had lunch, made some phone calls, and selected my outfit for the concert later that night.

Next I found myself being awakened by my cell phone ringing. I looked down at my phone to see Russell's picture on it. Now remember that Russell was away for the weekend for National Guard. Anyone familiar with the Armed Forces knows that if you're away for your weekend, you can't place or receive any calls during that weekend. So I knew immediately that there was a problem. I answered the phone, "Hi son," with hesitation in my voice, "Is everything ok?" Russell proceeded to tell me that Nikki had been in an accident at the home where she was babysitting, and that he didn't have any details, but I could call the owner on the phone to get some details and that he would meet me at the hospital.

I froze; I couldn't believe what I just heard!!! So Russell texted me the owners' phone number and I called them. At first the call rang and went to voice mail. I called right back and spoke with the husband and he stated that he had just arrived at the home and didn't have a lot of information, but he and his wife would meet me at the hospital. I dropped the phone and started to cry. I couldn't believe that my Sweetpea had been in an accident. Once I got myself together, I called Johnny and told him what happened to see if he could come and get me. He said that my Dad could probably get to me before he could so give him a call and he would meet me at the hospital. I called my Dad and when I told him what happened, he freaked out just like I did. Mind you Nikki's the only grandchild in our family. He said that he would be right over. That was the longest, heart & gut wrenching 45 minutes of my life! I paced back and forth, looking out of the window at every car that I saw and heard asking myself what is taking him so long? It's just a 15 minute drive!

When he pulled, up I ran out of the door not even sure if I locked it, told him to move over because I was driving. As I'm driving away I'm making phone calls to my friends (my sisters) telling them what happened and asking if they could meet us at the hospital.

Everyone that I called all had the same question, "Oh My God no! What happened?" I replied the same way, "I'm not sure yet. I won't know until I get there just please come if you can." As I'm making my calls, my Dad just kept saying to me, "You're not supposed to be on the phone!" I just looked at him and kept on doing what I was doing.

Once we arrived at the hospital emergency room, I saw the owners of the home where Nikki was. They informed the staff that I had arrived. A nurse approached me and asked if I was Nikki's mother I said yes. She told me that I could come back and see her, but only me. I told her that my Dad would be coming with me and she said that he couldn't. The Chaplin overheard our conversation and he said that it would be ok if he came with me. I said thank you. He escorted us into a family room down the hall to wait to speak to her doctor. I knew this wasn't good. The Chaplin introduced himself to us and informed us that he would be on call 24/7 as long as Nikki was hospitalized.

About 15 or 20 minutes later, Nikki's doctor came in to speak with us. He began to explain that Nikki had been involved in a drowning accident, and that they didn't know how long she was floating face down in the water, and if she was going to have any brain damage! At that moment I felt like I was in a Charlie Brown cartoon hearing the voice of his teacher.

A few seconds later I came back to reality and I asked, "I'm sorry did you just say they found my daughter floating face down in the water and that she might have brain damage?" The doctor said that they were not sure about the brain damage, but that they were going to run more tests to see what was going on with her. I fell to my knees yelling and crying, "No God! No God! This can't be true! Not my Sweetpea!!!!" My Dad did the same. The Chaplin and the doctor escorted us to see Nikki, and when I walked into her room I couldn't believe my eyes. I started to cry instantly. There was my Sweetpea laying in a hospital bed on a ventilator, with an IV, hooked to a heart & blood pressure monitor in a coma! I fell to my knees by her side! Once again I said, "No God! No God! No God! Not my Sweetpea!!" This time my Dad yelled, "No God, take me instead not my sweet sweet grandbaby!! I just lost my wife and my sister now you're taking my grandbaby!?" I snapped and told him that he needed to get out!!!

By this time a very good friend of mine had gotten there; she talked me off the ledge and explained to me that my Dad was also hurting and that I shouldn't have sent him out. So she went and brought him back into the room. About an hour later, I tried to contact Nikki's Dad but wasn't able to reach him so I contacted his Dad and told him what happened and where we were. He said that he would let Nikki's Dad know what happened.

Shortly after I contacted Nikki's Grandfather, other friends, family, and church members started to arrive. The nurse came to me and told me that they were about to move Nikki to ICU and that I could ride with her, but everyone else would have to meet us up there. So I relayed her instructions and they met us on the ICU floor. I held Nikki's hand the entire time kissing it and telling her that I loved her. Once we arrived on the ICU floor, the nurses told me that they were going to get her settled and that they would come and get me. I left and went down the hall to the family room. When I arrived I couldn't believe my eyes. There had to be about 50 people there already and they were still coming! Everyone had the same question on their minds - what happened?!!! I didn't know what to tell them because I didn't know myself. We all decided not to dwell on what happened but to start a prayer circle and phone tree instead. Hours passed and the crowd grew larger and larger. When I realized it was 2:00 a.m., I told everyone to should go home and get some rest. I stayed there every night and day for 4 ½ days. Little did I know that my life would be changed forever that evening.

On Saturday May 30, 2015, I was awakened by Nikki's nurse saying, "Good morning, we need to change her. You can come back in a couple of hours when visiting hours start again." That's how the next 3 days were; the nurse coming in every morning and me not stopping for food. So I left and went back to the family room where my Dad was. Russell and his Mom were going home to go get changed and get something to eat. My Dad said that he was going to do the same and that he would be back later. I called Johnny and asked him to bring me some clothes also. By the time I finished speaking with Johnny, visiting hours had started again and I could go back and spend time with my Sweetpea! I went and sat by her side and started talking to her, rubbing her head and hand telling her that I loved her. About an hour after that her nurse came in to check her vitals she stated, "No real change, but we're going to run some tests later on this afternoon to see what's going on. The doctor will come by later to tell you what the procedure will be." She also stated that Nikki was getting the best care. That gave me comfort in knowing that my Sweetpea was getting the best care possible.

About an hour later a lot more family, friends, and church members started to arrive bringing lots of food. And my Dad, Russell, and his Mom had returned. Johnny had also come back to bring my clothes so I could shower and change. When I returned, Nikki's close friends Mom asked if I had eaten yet and of course I hadn't. She fixed me something to eat and took my phone informing me that I couldn't have it back until I finished all of my food. I flashed back to being a 3-year-old with my mother. While I was eating, she answered my phone, and took messages. So I did what I was told and finished my food so I could get my phone back.

A few hours later, the doctors came in to speak with us about Nikki. They informed us that they were going to perform a procedure where they froze her entire body for 24 hours, then they would slowly bring her body temperature back to normal. In doing this procedure, they would be able to determine if there was any brain activity. I had a million and one questions going through my mind, but I decided to wait to ask them. So at 5:00 p.m. on Saturday they started to freeze my Sweetpea.

Once they started the procedure, I went to the family room to thank everyone for coming. I met a lot of Nikki's youth church members (252) and a lot of the Elders from her church. I couldn't believe how many people came out to support my family in our time of need. It really brought a smile to my face because it reaffirmed to me that I had done a great job raising my Sweetpea.

A few more hours passed and more people came to visit Nikki. The crowd grew to about 300 or more people; I couldn't believe how many people were there to see Nikki. And as everyone knows, when a patient is in ICU you are only allowed to have 2 people at a time. Needless to say we exceeded that number! We took over the floor. The entire hospital staff was very accommodating to us and they allowed us to have 4 people at a time in Nikki's room. As more time passed, I realized that it was getting late again so I told the kids that they should get ready to go home. They all agreed and left for the night. It was about 2:30 a.m., so I returned to my Sweetpea's room to try to get some sleep.

On Sunday May 31, 2015 I went down to the family room to see if my Dad was awake yet. He was drinking some coffee from the day before. I asked him if Russell and his Mom were there, and he said that they left to go and shower so they could go to church and that they would be back later on that day. I asked him if he would be leaving to go home, and he said, "No I brought clothes for the rest of the time that Nikki will be here." I was glad to hear that he wasn't going anywhere. I didn't want to be by myself while I was waiting for visiting hours to start again. I went and showered and changed my clothes.

Once visiting hours started again, I went and sat with my Sweetpea. I liked going right in when they first started because it afforded me the opportunity to be alone with her because I knew as the day went on, she would have a lot of visitors. Around 11:00 a.m. people started coming in and so did the food again!!! This time I made my own plate and ate it before Nikki's Mom's friend got there. I also made sure that my Dad ate something because he wasn't eating either. After the last service at Nikki's church, a lot of her youth members, pastors, the Pastor's wife and a lot of their Elders came. We all talked and prayed together. We talked about how Nikki looked like she was getting better.

We thought that the machines indicated that her vitals were good. We thought that she was actually breathing on her own. Later we found out that wasn't the case. They went in and prayed for Nikki, left her gifts, cards, jewelry etc. There was always spiritual music playing in Nikki's room. As the days came and went, I began to get this overwhelming feeling of peace. At 5:00 p.m. on Sunday, they began to bring Nikki's body temperature back to normal.

Once they started the procedure of warming her body, everyone proceeded into the family rooms and the hallway. We had praise and worship with music and prayer, and the kids sang all of Nikki's favorite songs; people also rededicated their lives to God. As I looked around that room and into the hallway, I had a conversation with God. I said, "God if it is your will to take my Sweetpea, I'll be a peace." I felt a huge weight being lifted off of me and I found my peace in that moment. We lined all of her youth members in 1 single file line along the wall so they could go in 4 at a time to see her, talk to her, pray for her, or just sit with her if they wanted to. I was able to console the kids after they prayed for Nikki if they needed it. I actually sat in the hallway with one of her youth members for an hour or more rocking him in my arms. A few more hours passed, and it was 3:00 a.m. I had everyone leave so we could get some sleep. I went and spent my quality time my Nikki before I tried to get some sleep.

On Monday June 1, 2015, I went and showered and changed my clothes, and then I went to the family room to check on my Dad. We sat and talked and waited for visiting hours. By the time visiting came, her Dad and his fiancé had gotten there, along with Russell and his Mom. Her nurse came in and gave us some devastating news. She informed us that we had been reading the machines wrong the whole time and that my Sweetpea was never breathing on her own!!! We had been mislead by the staff. She apologized for the misunderstanding; she also explained to us how her machines actually worked. This is when we all realized that Nikki _came into the ER_ not breathing on her own. I was completely devastated!!! She told us that Nikki would be receiving a CAT Scan and an MRI, and depending the prognosis, that would determine what we would need to do next.

So we waited and prayed for a good prognosis. At 12:53 p.m. on

Monday June1, 2015, I was told by Nikki's doctors that she was pronounced **BRAIN DEAD!!!**

And on that day, the worst day of my life, I honored my Sweetpea's decision to donate her organs. She was such a loving and giving person, so what better way to give life than to preserve another's life? She saved a total of 5 lives. In an ironic twist of fate, my best friend's sister, whom I known for over 35 years, needed a heart. She received Nikki's heart which was a 100% match! Another friend of my Fiancé's received one of Nikki's kidneys which was also a 100% match! I get to hear my Sweetpea's heartbeat even though she's gone. Talk about blessings!!

A month after Nikki's passing, two of her youth members came to me with an idea to continue her legacy. We sat in Panera Bread on July 9, 2015 and started the "Smile For Nikki Foundation." We are a non-profit organization seeking to embrace others and enrich the community through the education of the performing arts, by providing training and mentorship for children in various facets of performing artistry. We enrich the minds of children ages 6-13 by providing training and performance opportunities in the arts of dance, vocals and acting.

I wanted to leave a note to other mothers who have lost a child or children. I know that you will never get over the pain of your loss and no one can ever know how it feels unless they have experienced it. But I say to you -keep God first and foremost in your life, surround yourself with positive people that can motivate you, and just take it moment by moment, hour by hour and day by day!

My greatest gift

12

You Will Not Break Me!

Winter Whitehorn

Winter Whitehorn is a confident, optimistic, intelligent, independent, strong, and powerful woman. She is a full time Bus Operator at the Chicago Transit Authority, an Author, Motivational Speaker, Life Coach, Time Management Coach, Self Actualization Coach, Financial Advisor, Project Planning Specialist, and Research & Information Specialist. As a single mother of two beautiful children, she has experienced so many trials and tribulations. Those experiences help her become who she is today, and she will not be broken. The issues that she has overcome in life are her journey toward enlightenment, and she embraces it with all her heart. She will ride the wheels of this thing called life all the way to the top, even if the wheels fall off. She wants to be an example to many women, showing them that there is no limit to success and that you can accomplish anything in life under any circumstances. She loves to immerse herself in new experiences and connect with other people. Right now, she is going with the flow of life and accepting all that it has to offer, meeting amazing people, and having amazing experiences. She am happy. She is also currently working on a seven series book called the "I AM" collection. Laugh, Love, Live Life.

Email: winterwhitehorn@yahoo.com

All I could here is the sound of a horn blaring, "Buuum, buuum, bum, bum." A lady swearing, "Bitch are you crazy? You must don't like yo life? Get yo ass outta the street!" she yells, as she turns the corner like a bat outta hell. I felt a whiff of air on my left leg. I looked up, the light was red and there was a 'no walk' signal for me. I had been in a zone on my jog like always when I'm plotting, planning, and thinking of my next move, reflecting on what I have accomplished, and what I wanted to accomplish. I was motivated, excited, and enjoying my life at this time. I was optimistic, independent, beautiful, intelligent, and successful in all the things I set out to accomplish. So, I looked around with a wide grin on my face and asked myself the question, "What's next?" Yes, I had almost gotten hit by a car while in my zone, and yes to the bitch who yelled to me about liking my life. I like my life very much so - in fact, bitch, I love my life. I was powerful, I was in control of my life, I was a creator, and my life journey reflected that. But, it wasn't always this way.

I started to call my chapter "Winter's Wonderland" because just like the fairytales we've all grown accustomed to, my life was like a fairytale that grew into an uncertain reality. Anita Baker,

sang it best in her song, "Fairy Tales," where she says, "...the story ends, the story's through, reality steps into view, no longer living life in paradise, no fairy tales." When I was a small child, my mom had this thick book of fairy tales like Cinderella and Snow White. Every night, she read one of these stories to my siblings and me. I thought my life would be like a fairy tale, but I soon came to realize this would not be true. As I grew up, I watched the women in my family take on their roles and responsibilities as being a mother and a wife. I also saw the men in my family embrace their roles as father, husband, the provider, and the protector.

> *When you're a child, these things are passed down to you through examples, and you begin to mimic and believe that this is how life is going to be for you. But as you grow up, you realize that it doesn't turn out that way for everyone. I am a prime example of this realization.*

When I was 18, I became with child. I finished high school where I meet her father. We will just call him baby daddy #1. I thought that he would be my Knight in shining armor; there's the fairytale thing again. I began to be the mother that I thought I was supposed to be and be his play wife. I looked forward to him getting a job and taking care of us, so I moved in with him and his family. He was on the basketball team when we were in high school, looking forward to being a big basketball player. However, that dream didn't pan out for him either. After a while, he grew depressed and sort of angry at me, blaming me for messing up his life so he quit school, never got a job, and started hanging out in the streets, and then he began to go back and forth to jail.

One day while I was getting my daughter ready for bed, his mom came into the room. In an irritated and harsh tone, standing in the doorway of my room with her right hand on her big hip and her lips tightly pressed together, she asked me, "What are you planning on doing with your life?" She was a healthy woman and she had a lot of rolls to support that hand. The ugly mushroom she wore for a hair style over and over again was played out too. Looking at her confused, I answered, "I don't know. I thought I was doing what I was supposed to do, being a good mom to your grand daughter and being a good woman to your son." She looked at me for a moment with her mouth opened as if she was shocked by my answer, and she said, "I think it's best you go back to live with your family," then she just walked away.

The next week, I moved back with my parents. At the time my daughter's father was in jail; he had six months. Every Monday, I took my daughter down to Cook County jail to see him. Again, I thought I was being a good woman and I wanted my daughter to know her father. When he was released, he continued the same behavior. When he came to the house to see me one day, he and my father got into a disagreement. My father wanted to know when he was going to be a man, acknowledge he had a child, and get a job. After the disagreement, my father asked him not to come to the house anymore. I went to my mother and asked her, "How do you think he's going to be able to see his child if he can't come over?" Mother, always so primmed and pressed with a fresh coat of nail polish to match everything she wore, tall, slim, and always in heels looked me straight in my eyes and said, "Honestly, I don't care. He doesn't need to see her if he's not taking care of her. I think it's best if he don't come over so you can get yourself together too. What are you planning on doing with your life?" Is this a trick question again? I stood there dumb founded. She continued, "Your dad and I will be there as much as we can for you but you're going to have to go back to school and eventually, get a job so you can take care of your daughter." I said, "What do you mean? I am taking care of her. Getting a job is not my job; I'm the mother." She looks at me with a serious facial expression and said, "It is now because her father is not going to do it." For the next few days, I stayed in my room with my daughter trying to stay quiet and out of the way.

A month later my mom came into my room and told me to get dressed. As I rode with her in the car she explained to me that she was taking me to get registered for school. She apologized for not being a better example, and she told me not to ever let my daughter think she had to depend on a man. I actually enjoyed school but went off and on because I continued to sneak and see my daughter's father. He would tell me he loved me and he would change, but of course, he never did. He went back to jail and when he came home I had gotten pregnant by him again.

The day when I walked to his house to tell him I was pregnant again, I saw this light skinned girl with long black hair down her back who I went to high school with; her name was Lela. She was there on his porch sitting on his lap. As I walked up everyone had gotten quiet. I asked if I could speak to him, and he looked at me dead in my eyes and said, "No. I don't think my woman would like that." "Your woman?" I repeated, confused because I was the one carrying his child and had his daughter. He asked if I could leave from in front of his house because he didn't want to upset Lela while she was pregnant with his baby. I stared at them for about ten seconds breathing hard. All of a sudden I saw myself lunge at them, Lela's long black hair wrapped around my left hand and me punching her in her face with my right fist repeatedly saying, "Now smile at this ass whoopin. You knew this was my baby daddy, bitch!"

He walked down the steps in front of me, then snapped his fingers, "Hello? Wake up, snap out of it. Did you hear me? I'm with Lela now. I don't want to talk to you. Can you please leave?" Damn, I was day dreaming about kicking her ass, but when I finally snapped out of it, honestly I wanted to cry, beg him, and ask him why but I didn't. I turned around and walked away with my head held high. Plus, I didn't want to make him mad. Embarrassed because everyone we knew was out there, I felt so stupid and my

heart hurt so bad, but it was nothing I could do but go home and cry. My heart felt like someone was holding it and squeezing as tight as they can and my stomach was upset.

The next day I went and asked my mom if she would help me get an abortion. The next week she took me to Planned Parenthood and I was scheduled to have an abortion that same week. I thought everything would be fine, but for two days following the procedure I had a hard time getting around. Afterwards, I cried every night for about two months and that third month I decided to stop being scared, stop feeling sorry for myself, and get up and do something. I went back to school and after a month, I met another guy from my English class. We'll call him, baby daddy #2. I found out that he was also an aspiring basketball player in high school. Before I met him, he had actually received a scholarship but before he was scheduled to go away for school, he was in a terrible car accident. He had to learn how to walk and talk again and when he did recover, they gave him a chance at his scholarship but he continued to get in trouble because of his anger of not being able to perform like he used to. He wound up at the Community College that I attended, Kennedy King. Two months after us hanging out, I had gotten pregnant by him and a month later he started hanging out in the streets and there goes a continuance of lies I fell for. The first lie was always, I love you. I was always a sucker for those words.

I finally got a job as a school bus driver, an apartment, and a car. One month later he crashed the car. He even started to get verbally and physically abusive. It lasted for about a year because I didn't want to have two children and not be involved with neither one of their fathers so I stayed. He would push me, choke me, lock me in the bathroom from time to time, harass me while I'm sleeping, whispering in my ear that he would kill me.

He would go on a rampage off and on tearing up the house, breaking my things, destroying my clothes, and punching holes in the wall. One time he hid me and my daughters clothes in three different abandoned garages and walk me through on the cell phone how to find them in the dark. It was torture, but I didn't think too much of it because at least he wasn't sending me to the hospital. When my son was three months old, he attacked me and almost stabbed me to death. Luckily, his sister was there yelling at him. It was like his mind snapped, one minute we were arguing and the next minute I was running around the kitchen dodging a knife. Finally, his faced changed from a raging lunatic to "What in the hell am I doing?" He ran out of the house saying, "Let me get outta here before this bitch have me going to jail for killing her."

I had been getting ready for a job interview when he accused me of sneaking on the phone with a man and snapped. Later I found out that he was diagnosed with schizophrenia after he had attacked someone else and was committed into a mental hospital. I left and went to a shelter. After three days of the shelter, I went back to my parents' house. That same day when he almost killed me, I had an interview with the Chicago Transit Authority for as a Bus Operator position and I missed the appointment, so the lady at the shelter called them and ask for an extension for me.

The next week I was interviewed, hired, and started training. I made the choice not to date anymore and get my shit together. In the first years the job was hard, there were constant up and down schedules, long swing shifts, and small pay. It was then when my mother started complaining. She said, "I don't know what's going on with your job, but I have a life too and I can't be at home all day with your children. You need to put the kids in day care." Because the government said I made too much money, I had to pay the day care myself, out of pocket. I definitely couldn't move out by myself, especially with my scheduling. We had what they call an 'on call' schedule where you didn't find out what you were working for the next day until 6:30pm the day before. Sometimes when you called in for your schedule, the line would be busy and you didn't find out until 8 or 9pm that you had to be back at work at 3am when you just left there at 7pm. Now, you have to figure out at 9pm who was going to watch your children, how they were going to get there, and what time you had to get up in order to get everyone ready, drop the kids off, and make it to work on time. Sometimes on the weekend when there was no daycare, I would ask my mom to watch them and when I woke up to get ready for work, she was gone for whatever reason.

As I became desperate for child care in order to keep my job, I would leave my children in the care of many people and pray that they would be safe. While I was at work, all types of things would play in my mind about my children. I thought about my children being abused or molested and some of the people I had to leave them with stayed where children were getting killed by gun fire while playing outside.

People at work kept encouraging me to stick with the company, everything would get better, and when I become full time, after a while, I would be able to pick my schedule and make more money. I needed that since I was the sole provider for my children. The thing is that it took 6 years to become full time. After 3 years of this mess, I decided to go back to school and obtain my Associates of Art degree in the hopes of moving up in the company and making more money. But it felt like the more I tried to move forward, I was set back ten steps. My son had started acting out when he was 4 years old and I had to spend more time and attention on him, taking him to and from counseling appointments. I just closed my eyes, kept moving, and hoping for a change. It was a hard, going to school full time, working extra hours, cooking, and cleaning up behind the children so I wouldn't hear my mom complaining, doing home work, helping them with their homework, spending time with them, doctor and dentist appointments, grocery shopping, washing clothes, and sometimes having to sit up at his school. It was a lot, and I was tired wondering why I was doing all of this and had nothing to show for it. Not being able to afford a place of my own, I just closed my eyes, kept quiet, and kept moving. There were days I didn't get any sleep trying to finish homework or just being worried about my children's safety, and how everything would work out. One day I went to the doctor and was told my blood pressure was too high and I had pre diabetes at age 31. "Are you serious?" I thought I was too young to be going through this and now extra stuff was added to my plate - extra appointments to learn how and what to eat and extra research as if I didn't have enough drama and stuff to do.

At times I was so busy or exhausted, I would forget things, like the time I forgot to set an appointment for the kids' physical and my daughter had to miss days of school until she got one. When I called to make an appointment, they didn't have anything available for over a month, so I had to call around to several places until I found this doctors office up North that told me if I could make it up there by 5pm they would take her as a walk in. Long story short, I started walking and I became so desperate that I flagged down a school bus driver and begged her to let me ride about 10 blocks with her, and she agreed. As I rode the bus with her I explained to her what was going on while starting to cry and she assured me that everything would be ok. When I made it to the building, it was 5:50pm and my legs were sore. As soon as I walked in the door the lady at the desk said, "We are closed ma'am. You will have to come back tomorrow." Tearing up, I explained to everything that I had gone through. She paused for a minute, held her hand out for my paper work, started taking my daughters vitals, and ushered us in a room. Seconds later, a small hunched over old lady came in, introducing herself as the doctor. She looked at my daughter and said, "So this is the little princess that needs her physical." My response was, "Yes, and thank you so much for seeing us." She turned and looked at me and said, while winking her right eye, "You made it just in time. I finished my appointments and decided to stay until 6pm for whatever reason but all that matters is that you made it."

Sometimes at night I would cry and pray so hard but when I woke up, everything was the same and still no help. Because of those hard times and painful situations, I became good at managing my time, and dealing with people and relationships. I learned how to research things, and also became excellent in dealing with my finances and budgeting. I had managed to increase my credit score to 820, pay off all my bills I created when I was with baby daddy #2, and save $15,000. In 2012, I turned full time and I applied for a house to be built and was approved. By that time, I had become an excellent manager of my life and all I had to do now was remove my children out of a bad environment. I purchased all types of tutoring programs to make sure they were up to par with their education. I made sure the area had high school scores, low crime rate, no pedophiles, and several activities for children.

My fairy tale had ended, my fairy tale was through, but I realized that my story wasn't through. I began my journey and it was long and hard, but it helped shape me into the person I am today.

Reflecting back on that journey, I wonder at this point in time, "What else can I do?" I went back to school and received my Associate of Arts degree and I was able to land the job that I currently hold as a full time Bus Operator at the Chicago Transit Authority for nine years, now, which allowed me to be able to take care of my children as a single mom as if they financially had a two parent household. This is why I stand at this crossroad with a big grin on my face after almost being hit by a car. I attend Toastmasters meetings to become a competent communicator which will allow me to possibly move up in my company or maybe even open other doors. I am part of several positive social groups. People are always asking me for advice and for me to research things. I am also writing a 7 series book called the "I Am" collection. Now, I stand here at  the crossroads with more options available to me with strength, courage, and determination. I am finally happy. I feel complete. I am having the time of my life and meeting amazing people. I now know who I am.

54794022R00100

Made in the USA
Lexington, KY
29 August 2016